POETRY
REFLECTIONS
AND OTHER
WORLD SCULPTURES

BY STEPHEN ROBERTS

Other Books by Stephen Roberts

Soulshift

The Stillness at the Edge of Time

Awareness

A Thousand Ways to Listen to Silence

Waking Up on Planet V (forthcoming)

Staring at the Wild Moonlight

"I think I will go downstairs and fill my glass with the mundane, fluff my rainbow pillow, and lie down on my unslept-in bed (the one with the neat hospital corners), trying to forget the footprints of the phenomenal lighting up all around me."

From my poem Footprints of the Phenomenal

"Some kind of celestial event. No — no words. No words to describe it. Poetry! They should have sent a poet. So beautiful. So beautiful... I had no idea."

— Dr. Ellie Arroway (Jodie Foster) in the 1997 movie Contact

A Soulshift Publication

Dedication

To you *the reader*—may your life journey continue to transform your world, over and over and over again. May it be a beautiful shaking, a delightful wounding, a profound awakening, a grace-filled drowning in the wonder of all that pertains to life.

To you *the poet*—I will never forget the day I read your words and something broke open deep inside. It may not have been your exact words or even your poem, but it was one of your kind—a poet, ancient or modern, and they were able to somehow remove a terrible deafness from inside my head and cause me to hear afresh in a thousand different ways.

May all you beautiful ones find an ever increasing rest as you experience the depth of *illumina*.

Poetry Titles

Reflection Titles

Big Pieces of Furniture

"Nothing remains as it was.
If you know this, you can begin
again, with pure joy in the uprooting."

Judith Minty, *Letters to my Daughters*

Back in 1964, novelist Susan Sontag wrote that "writing is a little door and some fantasies, like big pieces of furniture, won't come through." Sontag was aware that only a fraction of her soul was available to be turned into art. Only a fraction of what I really want to say in this book will seep through the words you're about to read. At times it will be joyous, delightful, almost humorous; at other times it will come with some exploration of pain, loss, and darker memories. To be honest, I still have a deep ache inside. I'm guessing it is spiritual in nature and that maybe you've experienced it also. I have a million questions about a million things and poetry is where I bump into some of the furniture.

I've often wondered if it is some sort of poet's disease; of being stranded somewhere between beauty and sorrow with no words that adequately express the emotions you experience, to others or even yourself. I find that I might just be moving Sontag's 'big pieces of furniture' around inside my head, hoping that if I move that old wooden chair closer to the window everything will be better. The ache is not so much a despairing lament, nor is it a crippling despondency (though one must be careful even here to leap to self congratulatory slaps on the back that everything is okay), it is more a longing to reframe my entire world without the sticky mud of past thoughts and spiritualities clinging to my words. My evolving beliefs are paving an exciting way ahead and all the curious meanderings of my soul have been a delight to experience, but the river is still flowing and the undertow is ripping the previous 'solid' sands of certainty from under my feet. We move ever onward.

I would say many creatives: poets, artists, musicians, writers etc., struggle with some visitation of a dark cerebral Cthulhu. Its tentacles seem to inhabit keyboards, typewriters, brushes, chisels, guitar strings, ink blotters, and lined paper pads. We wrestle with fears and forsaken hopes trying to get out that which is hidden within, and then, when a little flow of words does trickle forth, they come out all wrong, deformed by the need of trying to impress with pompous frills or banal verbosity. This book is about that fraction of my soul that I currently have available. It will be deeply poetic in parts for that mode serves my purpose to articulate the darkness of light and the light of darkness, these being the themes of growth and transition.

Consider this: here we all are, floating through space in what appears to be the middle of a vast and glorious nowhere, and all our perceptions of reality are woven with profound paradox and mystery. I hope this does not sound too weird or esoteric, honestly it is not meant to be, it is merely an exercise in 'poetic therapy'. You get to sit in on some of the sessions as my soul lies on a plush couch and looks up at the painted ceiling and talks to itself.

So much of what was presented to me as real in bygone days I now see as myth. And by myth I do not mean the popular misconception of falsehood. Nor merely "misunderstood history… nor diabolical illusion… nor priestly lying… but at its best, a real unfocused gleam of divine truth on human imagination." (C.S. Lewis) This refocus is disturbing to many, and rightly so. No one cherishes their most valued beliefs being classified as myth. Of course some aspects were indeed false and needed to be discarded, but whose fault is this? Was it the spiritual teachers and authors, all those dear mentors that spoke and instructed me with sincerity, dedication, and commitment?

No, I don't think so. I place any blame firmly on my own lack of seeing—a kind of stubborn refusal (and hidden fear) to *unsee* what I was told was the only correct way of viewing the world. I am reminded here of the wise words of Louis L'Amour, *"There will come a time when you believe everything is finished; that will be the beginning."*

When the dust of any deconstruction of belief settles there comes a time of necessary reconstruction. You and I don't want to stay twenty years in a morbid desert of self—sifting, moaning and groaning, melancholic to the core with a knot inside our soul. No, you and I desperately need some living water, some gentle bliss, some kindness and peace to ripple across our consciousness from time to time, and we know a simple Christmas-style annual hug will not do.

We need the integration of deep felt meaning into our lives. If we thrive here it will be a balm to our cracked psyche; otherwise, we end up extremely grumpy with life (and with everyone else around us). We will be unkind to shop assistants, to the drivers of other cars as they pass by, even unkind to our family and ourselves. We will carry an anxious happiness that forces smiles. We may post on Facebook that everything is wonderful, all our skies are crystal and blue, and yet, late at night the soul-troll under the bed returns and messes up our fake world with a plethora of extravagant and depressing thoughts.

Those who understand what is at stake in a spiritual paradigm shift will understand what the mystic said to the hot-dog vendor, *'Make me one with everything.'* Humor aside, this book is also about this *union*. 'That they may be one as we are one,' was not a mere holy platitude from some obscure Judaean prophet some two thousand years ago—I believe it is the living, breathing heart of all that can be captured in defining human desire and fulfillment. Jean Vanier's book, *Drawn into the Mystery of God,* speaks of divine union this way, "Union not only transcends every political, social, cultural, and religious consideration and not only infuses them with ultimate meaning, but defines the very purpose of life itself."

Throughout this book your will find a collection of poems written over the last several years. It is a place where I distill some thoughts I have collected on aspects of the journey thus far. Some ideas may seem unrelated, somewhat sporadic, but they do circle round a central sun— that of the heart of divine love maturing in the realm of consciousness.

The themes of *Ilumina* include the entrance of the mystical into our conscious awareness, the 'perceptions' of non-dualism (The Perennial Tradition), the mystery of grace, the depths of divine love, the

abundance of poverty, and, to use a Sanskrit word, ardhana हखिोज—
meaning worship, adoration, or devotion that flows from such an
encounter. It also deals with darkness and deconstruction of former
beliefs and of awakening to a whole new perspective of life. It is my
belief that a divine unity does indeed exist behind all our apparent
divisions and dualities—even between God and the human soul.

One of the great Western mystics, Lady Julian of Norwich (1342—
1416), once wrote in her *Showings*, "The love of God creates in us such
a *oneing* that when it is truly seen, no person can separate themselves
from another person...in the sight of God all humans are *oned*, and one
person is all people and all people are in one person." I begin to explore
the implications of the resultant wonder that rises from such a seeing.
In doing so I am not ashamed to fuse elements of the fantastic, old
myths, compelling legends and tales, with a deeper reflection on truth
and the variety of emotions that may accompany the spiritual journey.

I have an increasing respect for the wonder of our imaginations, to
allow its wild winds to blow across all our impoverished ideas that
remain content with spiritual dryness and boredom. One can spout
waterfalls of prosaic truth, and yet be as appetizing as a dust sandwich.
The point of my poetry is to capture in some small way the imagination
and longings of the soul, especially of those souls in spiritual transition.

The words you read, in this respect, will delve into fantasy and myth,
but are undergirded by a deep appreciation for far more ancient
traditions. Tinny sounding spiritual poetry often rehearse tired clichés,
trite concepts, or rigid dogmas. They carry about a banal simplicity as if
it were a sharp sword and wield an equal lack of depth on which to cast
one's heart.

Whilst some righteous souls may cringe at my use of myth, even pagan
sounding myth, it is my belief that the mysticism of which I speak was
also prefigured in those pagan myths. They contain cosmic pointers, a
small glimpse at wonder beyond what was currently known.

Could there be an echo of a deeper reality therein?

I think so!

Remember deeper magic is always being broken, whether it be in Narnia, the chambers of Hogwarts, or even our very own hearts.

The language of the Divine is the language of mysticism. Thus, it is the language of metaphor, a language beyond language. The intellect carries its own forms; so also the wild currents of the imagination. I have woven poetry and story around these aspects of truth, emotion, and spiritual awakenings.

The language of religion (and I am using the word 'religion' here in a negative context as something that binds a soul up in an endless sea of moral codes, lifeless ritual, and spiritual pedantics) abducts the former and holds it hostage under a savage and crude light— imperial, perilous, violent, and law bound. It mimics love, verbalizes adoration, and breeds a faulty and truncated relationship with ones own faith tradition. It broods in the corner of its own house of cards, frustrated at its own betrayal of its grand verbiage, but never conquers the longing and hunger to that which it strives. It remains forever, eternally discontent, bound to speak volumes of spiritual sounding platitudes, quote oceans of Scriptures (whatever the faith and whatever the holy book you esteem), but never enters into the fire of one's own relationship to the divine life and nature at the heart of everything.

Whenever I speak of spiritual soulshifts or awakenings I am invariably speaking of 'burnings'. How strange it is that we can now burn, from top to bottom, from beginning to end, and yet remain a breeding ground for trivialities and the parroting of truth. We are aflame with the universe *that is*, while the ash of the universe *that was* drops about our dark and sooty feet. And all those jumbled thoughts, dry and withered like a potpourri bag of scented belief, find replacement. Once precious and clung to for dear life, these beliefs are tossed into the air to be carried away by the inevitable wind of *that which I never was*, leaving only *that which I truly am*.

There is a whole new set of emotions we then begin to contend with. The crude light of some of these poems is contrasted with the darkness of others. They are representative of these two universes experiencing the flame of transition and rebirth.

Imagination can also lead to an expansion of our awareness. We begin to see a new world by seeing it through the eyes of others. As beloved author and scholar C. S. Lewis once remarked, *"My eyes are not enough for me."* You and I are in need of something that transcends our proclivity to deify a separated and individual self. The tiny world of my ego, the one that seems to think its grasp of reality is rather profound, is but a small sliver of my perception. Failure to realize this dilemma means we lose part of our humanity. We stifle childlikeness and close the door to a genuine humility that can embrace a beautiful curiosity throughout all of life.

Mysticism is also a language of paradox, of where the dark is bright and the poor are rich, of where the howl of the divine hurricane is the pinnacle of stillness, of where the ocean of the universe is contained in a grain of sand the size of your soul.

Underneath the layers of our religious skin and tightly wound egos a world is waiting to break forth into the freedom it aches for, but it has often become the ill-fated victim of certainty and hearsay. Spiritual learning, theological investigation, teaching and knowledge, these are all wonderful things, but there is a danger hidden even in these important pursuits. My Facebook friend Caleb Miller said it perfectly when he wrote, "I'm just about sick of all the so called Mystics acting like theology doesn't matter and all the so called theologians acting like mysticism doesn't matter. You can't be one without the other, and nobody agrees on everything. Get over it." You can learn all you want about marriage or raising children from books, but when you are married and have children then that is another kettle of whales altogether.

That being the case, the mystical journey is ultimately beyond words so it fits smoothly into the velvet glove of the poetic, rather than the prosaic. As a poet I am forced to write poetically in a book such as this, not that I shun the art of prose and exactness, but the elegance of the poetic form lends itself to embrace part of the Mystery. Think of this as my beginning exploration of *theopoetics.*

And for those who want a textbook definition of what theopoetics is, try this: "Theopoetics is an emphasis, style, and positive concern for the intersection of theology with the imagination, aesthetics, and the arts, especially as it takes shape in ways that engender community affirming dialogue that is embodied in nature and transformative in effect." (The Association for Theopoetics Research and Exploration)

I prefer to write this way, especially of God and matters of the soul, at least for a season. I want the Divine to stay a mystery for you, rather than attempt to have that supreme longing of our hearts eventually so neatly packaged, solved, and ultimately ignored in the muddy estuaries of definable religion. Poet and monk, Thomas Merton, also recognized the importance of paradox when navigating spiritual experience. *"Desert and void. The Uncreated is waste and emptiness to the creature. Not even sand. Not even stone. Not even darkness and night. A burning wilderness would at least be 'something.' It burns and is wild. But the Uncreated is no something. Waste. Emptiness. Total poverty of the Creator; yet from this poverty springs everything."*

What a beautiful insight. Poetry allows us to wrestle out some sort of meaning in a couple of lines or the turn of a phrase, broken though they may be. Poetry is meant to be read slowly; one takes a long bath in the words as they soak through your tough and grimy soul-skin layers. We are on a journey of discovery. We will change and see afresh. Total poverty, yet total abundance; total abundance, yet total poverty—capturing this reciprocal essence in your heart and mind has always been the central orbit of an encounter with mystical traditions.

Another well known mystic, St. John of the Cross (1542—1591) once said, "Launch out into the deep." His poetry and studies on the growth of the soul are considered the summit of mystical Spanish literature. His 'launch out into the deep' is forever the desire of the soul that longs for more. The mystic Jesus was reported to have said the same to Peter when he had been fishing all night and caught nothing, and we know the story well. Peter, probably a little reluctant and frustrated, nevertheless obeys and an abundance of fish flood his boat. The deep is where abundance lies.

I have read a considerable amount of the theological and spiritual reflections of Bede Griffith, also known by the end of his life as Swami Dayananda ("bliss of compassion"). He was a British-born Benedictine monk and priest who lived in ashrams in South India and became a noted yogi. During his third year at university, he came under the tutelage of C. S. Lewis who became a lifelong friend. Griffith developed a profound love for literature, especially poetry, and saw the connection between the language of poetry and that of mysticism. He remained convinced of the importance of poetry as a way towards the realization of the unitive spirit in all things. In his book *Pathways to the Supreme* he thus writes,

> "My interest in my youth had always centred on poetry, especially the English Romantic poets, Wordsworth, Shelley, and Keats. It was they who taught me to look beyond the world of senses to the world beyond senses, the infinite and the eternal. Poets use language of symbolism which always points beyond the finite temporal world to the infinite and eternal. It was Jacques Maritain and his wife Raissa, who taught me to see the link between poetry and mysticism....both poetry and mysticism spring from the depths of the soul beyond the senses, but whereas the poet seeks to embody his experience of this inner mystery in words and images, the mystic seeks to go beyond word and thought to experience the hidden mystery from which all words and thoughts are derived."

The depths of the soul are, as Griffith rightly discerns, ultimately beyond the senses. We cannot forge some esoteric peace on the anvils of human effort alone. In the beginning, the middle, and the end it is always the profound mystery of grace that causes poets, spiritual seekers, and even non-seekers, to come face to face with a reality they never knew existed.

Yet often, despite all our tireless skills at devotion, discipline, bhaktimarga, prayer, fasting, rituals, pujas, worship, meditation, yoga, humanitarian service, or a host of other spiritual practices, we are still left alone, shivering from sheer soul exhaustion, frustrated with so little experience of the abundance we know is out there, seemingly just beyond our reach.

Our empty soul-boats bob up and down, afloat on the Sea of Life, dreaming of some experience that will validate the core of our existence. We long for more, we know it in our gut, and more is available, just not for us. Frustration and depression result. We press in harder, taking even bigger gulps of the divine, but we become even thirstier. *The deep* is where your soul is flooded, and needs to be flooded, with an abundance that no mere human effort could ever manufacture. Well respected spiritual teacher Adyashanti speaks of being "taken by a moment of grace and falling into a sense of life we have not known before, a life that is not separate from you, when life is actually an expression of something indefinable, mysterious, and immense." This *being taken* I understand as the *inrush of the flood*, it is a tribute to a divine grace always available to every soul on the planet. The deep is like a thunder that keeps rumbling in the silent caverns of the soul, echoing off our dark chamber walls, longing to give you a glimpse of the heart's eternal home in the palaces of the God who abides within.

As I began writing this book a friend of mine, Diana Robbins, gave me part of her manuscript of her book *Beautiful, Naked Light* to review. In the opening pages she quotes the famous Sufi mystic Rumi (1207-1273). *"There are naked pilgrims who only wear sunlight, do not give them clothes."* The voice of the mystics has always been a song playing to the world to lead them home to the profound love that lies at the heart of all things. Often, we want to clothe those on a different journey from ourselves with our dogmas, doctrines, priorities, rituals etc. I am not saying that change or transformation of belief is never essential, in many ways it is essential if one is to ever experience the promised deep.

Of course, belief will dramatically change, but allow Spirit to have his way with every soul, be a loving guide and a friend, not a spiritual bully stomping on the sacred ground of other precious souls with our own self-righteous agendas. Let others wonder around naked in the sunlight of divine love for a while and allow the sun itself to clothe them (and you) in the process.

Jokingly I thought of changing to a pen name for this book, *Paramatmananda* (Bliss of the Supreme Spirit), or in terms more relatable to some of us than Sanskrit—Joy of the Spirit. All of us have a desperate need for this bliss or joy unspeakable. The participation in any religious rat-race, crowded with its vast ranks of furiously dedicated athletes and equally devoted gurus, teachers, and other holy (and often obscenely wealthy) men or women, must finally come to an end—we need to discover a soul-rest beyond the mountains of grand theory we are forever scaling.

I am wanting to discover what lies at the heart of human longing and what it is that connects us to that which is beyond. What is at the core of spiritual hunger, our restless dreams, our fragmented hopes, and our diverse longings? Many years ago when I researched for my Masters Degree, part of my cross-cultural emphasis was the study of major world religions and in my research I discovered many precious things that spoke to the soul in the most sincere ways. The human soul continually changes and finds renewal, meaning, and purpose far beyond creed and holy book (as precious as some of those things may be).

I am also aware of the glaring dissimilarities and how fundamentalism (of any label, shade, or hue) strips away any hope of dialogue or loving respect and communication with those we deem (usually with suspicion) as 'the other'. Many of us become stuck in our religion (even if our religion is 'non-religion') and never experience the depths of divine grace and the restoration of a vital flow of life within. One's soul must begin to experience awakening, even a momentary flash of light will do, for any authentic healing or renewal to take us further on the path of light. Michael Meade identifies some of the pain and confusion that can accompany this awakening in his book *The Water of Life: Initiation and the Tempering of the Soul,* "Embracing a new way of being requires that aspects of the old sense of identity be sacrificed and left behind." Jesus himself talks about discovering a Self beyond the old self when he says, along with other great spiritual teachers, that there is a self that has to be found and one that has to be let go of or even "renounced". As we encounter an inner dying, we open to the possibility of an inner resurrection. Author and speaker Richard Rohr clearly makes this distinction when he uses the language of the True Self and the False Self in many of his writings. Rohr says, "Both True Self and False Self will feel like your "self," so you see the confusion. One might be called true 'centering,' and the other is the more common 'ego centering,' which shows itself to be the core of the problem."

In this book I wish I could promise you that you'll find all your questions answered, that you could download true inner peace like a new iPhone app, and even possibly have an out-of-body experience in which you meet with several wise and witty ascended masters. This is probably not going to happen, not even remotely, but what I can promise you is an unfolding of my own journey into the mystical dimensions of belief that have been ruminating in my eccentric soul over the last several years.

This may shock and scare some of my older friends that thought I was still on an easily defined straight and narrow path (well, according to their version of what they consider qualifies as straight and narrow). But here is a secret: we are all evolving, we are all in process, we are all discovering and rediscovering; hence, we are all redefining and reknowing. We are finding our eyes, some perhaps for the very first time.

We all experience our various spiritual baptisms, whether it is a silent faith crisis or the mighty high of a spiritual bliss-out. These all inform our mind and our interpretations of life. In the famous words of the 1965 hit by The Byrds, *Turn, Turn, Turn* (incidentally based on the ancient Hebrew book of *Ecclesiastes*), 'There is a time to be born, and a time to die,' there is a time for new perspectives to be born and there is also a time for old perspectives to die. A wise person once said, 'new wine cannot be placed in old wineskins'—in other words, new life cannot be contained in the old, hard paradigms of the soul.

Some of my readers already know that I was once a long time resident of a country called Fundistan, a fundamentalist land of mind and soul that required everything be squared away with absolute spiritual certainty or otherwise I might burn in a hell like some delightful little cartoons portrayed. I had my spiritual passport stamped, and I was a willing ambassador for their every creed. Every question had a spiritual answer, every demon had a Bible verse to kick it back to eternal darkness, and every tragedy had a sin-judging God behind it. I was not nice; in fact, most of the time I did not even get along with the me I had become. My mind was filled with borderline-hate literature and fire-and-brimstone books. I did not see it then—I would have called it 'the hard truth'—but then along came a faith crisis, in hindsight perhaps it would be better to call it a life crisis, maybe it was a theological crisis, or even an intellectual crisis, whatever it was, in the middle of all this something called divine grace appeared in my soul one day and the universe opened up in ways I cannot put in words, even to this day. This happened back in 2011-2012, and no, it was not due to the ending of the Mayan Long Count calendar. Nor was it an overnight 'aha' Zen like moment; rather, it was a gradual slow slide off the edge of the world I once knew. Gladly, I resigned of trying to understand God, and somehow I think God was a lot happier also, and guess what, I'm still sliding.

Does this predicament of spiritual deconstruction keep me awake at night wringing my hands over decades of lost spiritual ground? You may think, probably it does, but again, no; however, it does make me profoundly aware that our spiritual perceptions are still open to such incredible change.

If we can survive our great psychic plunge into a dog-headed-determination which often delights to sink its fangs into stubbornness and ecclesial security; if we are willing to wander into the wilderness where the wild winds of Spirit blow every hair from off your sacred head; if we allow the slightest sliver of light to shape fjords of magnificence within, calling us to deeper mystery and awe, then, I believe, incredible opportunities for meaningful growth and spiritual transformation are likely to occur.

One thing I know these days is that any notion of indefectibility from what you think is orthodox is held together by thin paper chains. There is a divine love, fire-like and burning, it is a flame of intensity, compelling us all forward into a matrix of the incredible and the impossible. It is not that you are venturing into error, but our little containers of truth are simply not big enough or strong enough to house all these insane and revolutionary ideas that keep popping up in your head. They are cosmic in scope, global in import, and transformative in life, they are also very difficult to muzzle. This is no excursion into a gray monotone of drudgery and useless epiphanies, it is the beauty of the universe cracking open, one grain of sand at a time.

You are aboard your little starship, and guess what, you will eventually hit the spiritual equivalent of the Van Allen Belt as you seek to go deeper into the Mystery. All the energetically charged particles of new insight will come at you from nowhere. The flashing red warning button in your head will suddenly go off in its own mad chorus of mindless beeping, illuminating your whole craft with a deathly red glow. And the little starship you thought was so sturdy and secure is now popping rivets and weld joints. You're shaking on route to a collision with new celestial realms, and you have no idea how to navigate in the dark, you don't even know where the brake is, and the trusty control column broke a few months ago.

See, you are not as strong as you think; nor are you as wise, as perfect, and as knowledgeable as you have told yourself. You will experience turbulence. Some of what I say here, though often like a bad in-flight documentary, may at least may explain some of the ways to strengthen your vessel and keep a little sanity in the process.

Once I thought I was the grand spiritual origami master folding paper doctrinal cranes in the basement of my studious soul. A little fold there, a well defined crease here, a tap, tap, tap with my index finger to make sure the beak was nice and flat and well formed for its long and perilous flight to eternity.

Life is a lot more—wait for it—*diverse* than that. It cannot be captured in the once simplistic assertions of truth we try to bottle and seal so elegantly. The continual tap, tap, tap of my index finger resulted in an arthritic and calloused soul. I had become systematic, mechanical, and cold. God had become cold, we had become cold together, yes, we were still friends, but chilly friends as our smiling glances saw each other at a distance. I wanted what the great Sufi poet Hafiz wrote so simply:

> *God and I have become*
>
> *Like two giant fat people*
>
> *Living in a tiny boat.*
>
> *We keep*
>
> *Bumping into each other*
>
> *And laughing.*

I had replaced simple trust with a frothing dogmatic certainty. I had reduced transcendent mystery to irregular verbs, petite nouns, and other archaic writings. I tried to define awe, instead of melting in its grip. Honestly, when one begins to define awe and live from that 'defining' I think they are poking around in areas that are psychotic to the soul. The ineffable was reduced to the best sectarian and regicidal statements I could muster. Fire and rain and wind and earth had been domesticated into a theological pot plant that I watered each week with a new set of spiritual sounding clichés.

Ah, but God is a wild forest, borne of fervent deep mystery, a roaring ocean of burning wonders, a tornado of spilling wind, and a gentle voice of dove like immanence. If this is the dimension that a 'faith crisis' called grace brings, then drown me in it.

I believe the true mystic shuns trite clichés and holds to that which cannot be explained. Not that they cease speaking of spiritual matters, but there is far less dogmatism lurking in the background of their trembling voice. The mystery is deeply known, but utterly unexplainable. The mystic can only drop little pebbles into the ocean of the universe, hopeful that one may cause a ripple that sends a flood of light in your direction. They form a bridge between worlds—between an ordinary and a non-ordinary reality.

I find the poetic voice extremely helpful here as a form of spirit-embodiment that does not want to dilute what it is attempting to describe. But to descend to mere definitions and dogma tends to shackle the imagination and form the seeds of fundamentalism and tribal sectarianism.

Let's climb out on a limb of the Tree of Life. Let's revel in the view we see, for it will be both intense and wonderful. But beware of gripping the branch with a white knuckled hope fearing a fall. Love knows no 'white-knuckled' grip on reality, it simply rests and releases knowing that even if we fall from the branch and plummet to the earth below, then even the very earth we land on is alive with the fire and the love you experienced above on the branch. The mythical turf is, in fact, all around us. It is *in us*, like the ocean flows through and surrounds a fish. We exist in a God-saturated, God-breathed cosmos. The inner fire you touched whilst clinging to the branch inhabits all things, and all things are held together by its beauty and power.

If there is such a thing as an 'old mystery' then the 'new mystery' will radically transform whatever we thought was so essential and concrete to the old. I think here of a Saul transformed to a Paul as one example of a 'mind-blown' man (see the Biblical book of Acts). He was once a religious terrorist and zealot, now a lover and friend of those he once wanted to silence. And I suspect there are still plenty of Sauls in every religion and ideology on earth.

Welcome then to the emphatic dynamism of life itself—especially our kaleidoscopic spiritual lives as we continue to encounter and embrace the Mystery. Yes, I continue to walk with the mystic Christ, the humble Nazarene carpenter who shook the religion, politics, social order, and beliefs of his day, so may our lives continue to experience an ongoing mild epiphany (no, let's make that a severe epiphany—and I am being kind here) as we attempt to walk our way 'naked in the sunlight of reality' as it is unfolded to each of us.

I want to leave you some thought-provoking questions that Brian McLaren poses to us: *"How do you think Jesus would treat Moses, Mohammed, and Siddhartha Gautama (the Buddha) if they came to a crosswalk together? Would Jesus push Moses aside and demand to cross first, claiming that his ancestor's failed religion had been forever superseded by his own? Would he trade insults with Mohammed, claiming his crusaders could whup Mohammed's jihadists any day of the week, demanding that Mohammed cross behind, not beside him? Would Jesus demand the Buddha kneel at his feet and demonstrate submission before letting him cross? Or would he walk with them and, once on the other side, welcome each to a table of fellowship, not demanding any special status or privileges, maybe even taking the role of a servant— hanging up their coats, getting them something to eat and drink, making sure each felt welcome, safe, and at home?"*

How we answer these questions tells us much about ourselves, perhaps more than we are really comfortable with.

May the peace you long for be yours in abundance as you awaken to the flow of *Illumina*.

Note: You will notice on one or two of the entries in the main text a source or inspiration credit, usually at the bottom of the page. For example, a Twitter reference (@twittername) or some other reference, indicates the origin of the quotation.

Stephen Roberts

April 2016

PLEASE

READ

SLOWLY

WELCOME TO

THE FANTASTICAL

THE MYSTERIUM

THE TREMENDUM

THE MYTHICAL

THE ENIGMATIC

THE ILLUMINA

¶ POETRIA

She scratched her black lines across a white page; a magical portent, an alchemy of the fantastic transmuting the dull base-metals of thought and grey memory into some rare poetic gold.

Sometimes she despaired language. Poetic lore seemed destined to struggle within its steel vernacular cage—an angel bard stripped of its majestic white wings, forever to slog the haphazard swamps on the bleeding feet of self-doubt, restricted metaphor, and clichéd epithets.

The danger of her poetic imagination was intense, like the violence of a winter storm. Allusions became thunder, phrases surfaced as rain-drenched eulogies to a deeper state of being, words leapt about on snow-driven winds—each striving for some calm with life and with death.

She was a priestess of thought, a mediator of the sacred, a seer of the forest of both delight and horror. Her verbal iconography hung like incense in the stone temple of her mind. She ascends mountain tops and assess the insanity of the world, seeing its boneless smiles and its incredible longings.

Deep sensory, divine knowing, melancholia and ecstasy—these be the kindling in her soul. The luscious glades of solitude invite a mystical piety, despite her being unable to live with her very uncertain self. Wild flowers carry the fruit of God, meadow-sweet and succulent, defying the mundane with a brief glint in their rainbow eye.

She also knows the nightmare lodged high in the cliff rocks. There the prophecy-birds nest and the dark ravens gather. She saw the battle of the trees and how they forged weapons of good and evil from the aftershocks of Eden's primal glow.

She is flesh without flesh, bone without bone, thought without thought—a wind looking for an earth on which to blow.

Yet in her often withered state, when green things tumble down to a brown earth, there lies a sprouting bud, hidden and quiet, nymph-like among the whispering forest. Beyond her tangled mind of twisting twig and battered branch a white fire prospers, mischievously robed in a golden sun.

Swift-flying do her words then come, fletched from the white-hot feathers of natures beloved armory. Bashful she becomes, tamed by the immediacy of her sudden words.

She: the fool, the stammerer, the banished one, destined to a dramatic seventy years of irrelevance on a mad earth.

But she is surviving: a poetess, a goddess, a crippled fiery myth burning in darkness.

She who was birthed by the moon is now clothed with the sun.

She divides the day from night with the breaking open of her words, and the size of the shadows somehow diminishes.

Leave her alone and she will startle you.

Invite her in and you will burn in the light of her gentle apocalypse.

¶ MOONBAKING

Moonbaking is advised for all nocturnal poets—
sky clad and soul full, creatures of this ilk
need to rest long in the milk rays of moonsets,
gently sipping the cream from wordless pages before the
audacious soaking seeps back into the quiet earth.

Her borrowed light,
a gilding silence,
whispering its way into the
solitude streams of your soul.

The tender places of the heart
delight in unhurried moon-time,
every single thought strangely gentled
by the waves of white light
breaking upon the sands
of your upturned face.

¶ TETRANYMPHON

The nymphs first came from their exquisite realms of metaphor and mystery like a gale. They, perfectly illumined in the evening light, shocked the haunts of my oft solitary mind so distracted and distanced by a lifetime of foolish speculation.

My shapelessness submerged—my mind slowed.

Why now, in my rabid uncertainty, do the hills and forests look infinitely green in their motionless wonder?

The first, *Aurae*, came as a blue dove-like shimmering—unnameable, exposed, naked like a mountain creek, wordless in ecstasy for no reason, and yet, every reason in the world I could think of gave rise to her bliss. The gentle air about her did not insult the soul, but contained a burning invitation. Her breath became a quill, and upon the petals of flowers did she write, though unaided by any hand.

THE AURAE PROPHESY:

'Sound and fury signify nothing,
smash the mirror gods,
embrace a deeper yes and
all will transform.'

The second, *Aegle*, a spring morning of unclouded light with crimson wings aglow. Down she came to sit by the oak tree, tracing the air with a smooth flow of golden tinted leaves. She came to tame my tongue from its immense bee-like buzzing. Her cheeks were the color of lilac, her eyes flashed in silence, fluttering about her were a vast array of singing raindrops with tiny wings.

THE AEGLE PROPHESY:
'In the great unlearning
many things hidden
will be revealed.
Impure poetry has the weight

of granite mountains and
blocks the bright star rising
in the east of your soul.'

The third, *Hyades*, came fresh from the stars with clusters of soaking rain clouds. Ah, what a glorious breaking overhead—tempests swell, Pleiades pours, preparing the ground for new sight. Sudden growth leaps with great force from where her feet tread. She told me she knows the names of a billion stars—*my sky-islands*—she called them, each burns with a blue fire that dazzles even the thoughts of the holy Seraphim. Somehow she communicates though she is noun-less and verb-free. She knows the verbosity of gods is useless on a deaf earth.

THE HYADES PROPHESY:
'Climb the stem of a flower
and you climb into the
very throne room of the universe.'

The fourth, *Naiads*, sprung from the deep, the eternal, the longing. Prometheus has abandoned the fireplace of the gods, exiled by a flood that covers the universe. His fragile ego a knee jerk away from haemorrhage. Naiads' lush waters rage in a universal flood—did you not know the sound of the ocean is an unplumbed majesty. She is everywhere an ocean, but she still burns in an unexpected flame.

THE NAIADS PROPHESY:
'Come, drink from my chalice.
Let your soul blush like a timeless pilgrim,
the air will become dense with truth-flowers,
and that fatal quest for perfection
will finally let go its stifling grip.'

❡ NAMASTE

"Do you believe in namaste?"
"Only if I spend at least ten hours a
day pretending the world doesn't exist
as it does," he said.

She said, "But what about the moon,
the stars, the rocks, and the flowers -
don't they drink the sun-fire breath of God?"
He said, "Only when I sit and think
myself out of all the shadows that have
climbed into my tiny soul cage."

"Ah, the dark infinities of mystery," she said,
"but even shadows long to break from the
ancient patterns of a million year brutishness."
He said, "Then I shall open my wounded chest
and allow all my dark words to tumble to the
floor—come, help me thaw this obsidian glacier,
the forests and tundra are in good need
of a golden gesture of affectionate light."

"Namaste," she said.
"Namaste," he said.

¶ TEA WITH TRINITY

It is never easy to let go of the earth you once knew. All the old trees and rocks still whisper, endorsing your hundred or so thundering thoughts. It seems the entire path to the stars is an intense journey littered with still another thousand ancient sages begging your attention.

I don't want to sound grandiose, but it is too damn easy to drown in the shallow end of life, missing the deep terrain that your soul delights to roam through. Inner kingdoms tend to have cryptic maps at the best of times.

So I want to sit down and have a good hot cup of tea with the Holy Trinity, I will pull out my finest doctrinal china (the pretty petite ones kept high in the tea cupboard)—long into the night we can discuss ethical logjams and worlds unseen over scones and peppermint aromas.

Later, after we have all ascended to bed, I will pull out my dusty tome of speculative formulations, the shattered cosmology of what I thought I knew, the physics of angels, the dharma of doubt, and all those tears I have bottled up for decades.

I will swirl the bottle in the esoteric moonlight and see if it turns the color of wild strawberries. I wonder if it will be as far off-limits as one can get. Will it overlap genius or madness—that eclectic synthesis of all the starlight ever poured over the lonely sighing mountains?

After the perusal of my soul-maps I will attempt a soul-salvage. Useless, yes I know, but therapeutic nonetheless. A frustrated nudge at inner awakening with my heart firmly placed in my mouth. Can the blind force a seeing? Maybe the ocean tides will flow again, recovering from its waste of static stoic sand.

Omega weds Alpha and back again. The Vastness, I can almost taste it. Spaciousness untrapped. *Consummatum est.* Cosmic imagination rekindled, intellectual integrity befuddled—the wingspan of deep space is slighter bigger that I imagined.

Am I adrift in some post-Jungian sea of archetypal waves? I giggle, then I think 'How unholy', looking at my primordial binary boat with the little wooden oars—the great polarities of left and right and right and wrong; of good and evil and life and death; of light and dark. I have yet to see mere moral behavior enlighten anyone.

What if tea with the Holy Trinity opened a great deep? An abyss. A benevolent breaking of the whole. A supreme and ultimate fusion of hot water, tea leaves and wonder. Enough at least to disturb my next 24 hours of thinking on reality, nakedness, and why the night wind hides it so well.

Life is a glass perfume, broken open. A sustaining fragrance. Even one skeptical whiff and you're intoxicated at the well of all time. It wafts into deep soul, carefully plotting the downfall of all that has been, rerouting wisdom and awareness and kindness and joy. You become planted in the bold and the spacious, and the utterly remarkable.

Sipping tea with the Trinity I was reminded we all have to pass through the eye of the needle. All your threads run loose and blow in the wild wind, unraveling from their cosmological cardigan like a scattering of autumn leaves swirled by an afternoon rainstorm.

I will keep a diary; deepening my soul dream over the next thirty years or so. It'll be my *Short Course in Wisdom*—small, staple-bound volumes, a little frayed at the edges, smudged with tears and memories. They will still have a lot of unanswered questions from when I was young, questions from a world that had not hurt me yet.

God, do you want another cup of tea?

ꝑ GENTLE THUNDER

When the soft small voice comes as gentle thunder in your soul, when its consuming majesty breathes its own sacred flame; yes it can be sweet and bountiful and immortal, and also absolutely terrifying.

Your serious and very proper adult world will begin to close in around you, tempting you to abort that strange line of reasoning. But, with imagination captured and a rare beauty burning, you will find yourself silently repeating these solemn words:

"Go gently,
go deeply, and
go humbly in the
way of love."

¶ THE MERMAID WAY

I am a mermaid,

see my ocean pour—

deeply I breathe;

wonderful, inexplicable,

is this drowning beauty.

I fear no depth,

only the shallows

where the scales of my soul

cannot sink, but only

wither and shrivel to sun dry white.

I am still searching for

the marvelous in the

worlds that are deeper down,

worlds that have yet to

pound an already wet earth

and say, "You're still not living yet."

¶ THE BIRTH OF A FAE

I wonder if their eyes are like reflected silver moonlight off a river at night?

I wonder if their faerie-pale skin shines in a translucent glow?

I wonder if, from the hour of their birth, their wings unfold in splashes of light?

I wonder if the long and slender limbs already know the touch of the deep forest?

I wonder if their soft breathing stirs the mighty oaks and ancient stones as they watch from the shadows?

I wonder if the color of autumn already spills its fiery shades of yellow and red across their tiny cheeks?

I wonder if the wild flowers bow gently to the earth to honor their arrival?

I wonder if the ever green leaves and soaking roots tremble at the news?

I wonder if the fae are close cousins to our souls?
I wonder if we will ever know?

The sense of the sacred is something pervading the whole order of nature. Every hill and tree and river is holy. Every ocean, mountain, and creature speak as prophet and sage. Even the simplest of human activities, such as eating or drinking, through to birth or marriage, are all sacred in character. Yet sadly, all around us, everything is becoming profane, cheap, banal and explainable. *Illumina* is about living in the sacredness of a pregnant *now*, it is knowing the sacramentality of the universe—that the whole creation is pervaded by God. Living in this moment, with this awareness beginning to nurture one's consciousness, with this sacred breath flowing into all your experience, this is what will revolutionize your entire world with beauty.

| *The Sense of the Sacred*

⁋ THE WATERS ARE DEEP, BUT I HARDLY KNOW IT

She was way too out-there for tradition,
too intellectual for the contemplatives,
and too mystical for the intellectuals.

So she sighed under
the bombardment of
her interior castle that was

too esoteric for the orthodox and
too orthodox for the odd—
she simply did not fit in anymore.

So she took an inner vote on reality,
feeling for a pulse beat on her academic vein,
"Ah, there it is," she cried, feeling strictly off limits

in her new paradigm of inklings.
Theoria and Praxis snuggled closer together,
like a lightning storm to a bright flash,

Maybe this explains why
she couldn't be explained and why
the twilight sky keeps on grinning

at her humble light and naked dark.
Things are changing in the great ocean
of the eclectic and wild, her curiosity

evokes blank stares as people try to
navigate her ley lines of mystery,
but the high mountain path of her soul is

still being mapped out by a sacred geometry.
And who knows, you might just encounter a parade
of fairies or angels or both—and that is sure

to make your head spin into a free fall as your
logical mind shrinks away in disgust, but
sobbing ever so quietly is

your great poetic heart,
grasping at first sight
what you were once so blind to see.

❡ SPEECHLESS

Blank faces stare
back at me
as I fumble
for the words
to explain
why the sun
has so burned
this trembling soul
in an ocean of light.

¶ COMMUOVERE

Sacred sight: one radiant light.

I open the book of the moon

and reflect.

There is always something deep within her skin.

Sacred surge: one untranslatable peace.

Enduring, embracing, enchanting, endearing.

The soul of the silk mind,

now with beautifully tears,

deepens its audacious smile.

Commuovere is a word usually lost in translation that comes close to meaning "heart-warming", but in the sense that it directly relates to a story that has moved you to affectionate tears. It is Italian in origin. The Hungarians also have a word like this, but I am not going to tell you what it is...it's a secret!

¶ SUN THERAPY POETIC

1.

Good morning heartache, am I desperate enough yet? The long, lonely walk into the listening forest is just the withdrawal I need today.

Is this the day I throw it all away? No, I will write one more poem, just to stay alive inside, hoping to infuse clarity into a single word.

What can I write to the profound wilderness? Do I have what I need to be free to feel who I really am? Am I a laboratory of emotion or an artist?

2.

Complacency and transformation tug at the soul like a fiery riptide, the twin polarities of apocalyptic power fiddle with the art of ascending.

There are so many things I am not allowed to tell you. I am still all broken, wearing a white porcelain mask. Is there a place where my painted smile can yet fall into grace?

The petals of my timid soul are innumerable, loose like the wind, thoughts wanting a reciprocal balance to swoon around some future imagined self.

3.

Why are the sun, the moon, and the stars so integral to my sanity? They have a cosmic wink, often cloudy, but certainly deep.

Not now, not yet, wait! The autism of terror cannot save, nor can a giddy infatuation with the small box of dark truth that poets carry.

At least the sparrows are sympathetic listeners—they sing at depression and hop from branch to careless branch over my spindly anxiety.

4.

I'm sitting at the back of the room, crying, a spiritual placebo rattles down my sunken throat, half unseen, alive, but desperately fake, like a torn cloth of hopeless warmth.

A spontaneous smile would be nice—'roses still bloom' I tell myself, for reasons they have keep secret for years—'they bloom, even on the graves of the dead'.

I am a chrysalis, flecked with diamonds I still cannot see. My soft skin a tomb, slowly I reach from its cage. Winged, but wingless—soaring with steel wings grinds the soul on the hard rim of the sky.

5.

Yesterday I felt a deep unease whilst staring into the sun. Oh great marmalade light on the hill, do you only burn and consume? Don't you have a kinder warmth waiting in your ocean light?

My soul sways on a great tidal abyss. Some call it the ocean, I call it the moon-driven sea, with darkness deep, but somehow the light still manages to drip down my cheek.

The portal of light often shakes the left hand of darkness. So never trust dark poets, not completely, the bizarre is often a dead place, opaque, condensed, and to be consumed like pepper.

6.

If lightning obscures the ground with a bright puddle of light then strike me over and over again. Is this why I am made of tin, a frame for something more heavenly?

I was always told not to look directly at the sun. It's sharp yellow arrows would pierce the foolish eye. A drunk Dionysos prefers to hide in his smiling cave of shadows and rage at the world.

Seamless warmth, white breath of light, I now hold my peace. Close your eyes and open your mind, labyrinths last longer in the frightened corridors of shadows, better to keep tattoos of the sun inside your flaming soul.

¶ QUESTIONS ABOUT
HEAVEN AND THE SILVER
WHALES OF NEPTUNE

Does Heaven have grey clouds
or do they billow daily in an
ever shiny puffy whiteness?

And what about the flocks of gigantic butterflies
with their marvelous rainbow wings—do they soar across
the rooftops of the houses of the dead?

Do they sit perched on back fences,
wings moving slowly to that
mysterious rhythm that is everywhere?

Do they sing sonnets to the tiny smiling flowers just
waking up to another eternal dawn?

Is the air always very still?

Is the air always very quiet?

Or is there a small rush above the sacred hush,
a careless whoosh of wind as angels slam their
apartment doors, flying to catch

the last silver moonbeam leaving for the
Celestial Throne?

Are there storms that engulf entire cities in a
sparkle of stars, twisting like gentle
clusters of sunset cyclones?

Do raindrops fall in brilliant colors,
soothing and healing those who endured
such vicious and cruel times whilst on earth?

And what about those angels who are working
late at airport immigration, do they always have
a kind word to say to those who are
finding it hard to make the transition,
never believing they would make it this far anyway?

Do your traveling bards always play wooden lutes
and harps or do they break out occasionally in
a wild flute solo trying to coax the gathering
woodland creatures into an impromptu jig?

Is there ever any litter on your streets of gold?
A rusty bottle top?
A strand of old string?
Perhaps a tiny sliver of broken glass or
a crumpled page from last week's newspaper?

Or do the streets always reflect that dance of fiery gold,

wafting the sweet fragrances of myrrh mingled with

exotic and rare spices (of which I

still cannot pronounce correctly)?

Do any of your blessed dead look after the biggest zoo

of the entire universe, with dragons, and unicorns,

and those little heard about silver whistling whales

that night dive the cool oceans to Neptune's core?

Or do all creatures roam wild and free,

populating entire planets without fear of

being hunted or eaten or suffering ever again?

Is there a great celestial library filled with

millions of flying books and scrolls?

Do I need to wear laced gloves?

Can I eat the pages?

Or do they consume me?

Is there a growing middle-class with that

inevitable urban sprawl through your

towering cities of light?

Do statues of generals still stand proud in your

downtown city parks, their polished steel faces

still shouting out of great battles won?

Or have you replaced them all with those
quiet, white swans that fly across Orion's Belt;
the ones who write peace poetry and fluently speak
the ten-thousand dialects of the Pleiades cluster?

Do you have underground railways that
tunnel through huge diamond mountains?

Do people help the elderly get on board
and find them a comfortable seat?

Come to think of it, do you even have 'elderly'
or is everyone exactly thirty years old
forever and ever, amen?

Do white children always play nice
with brown children, and do they always
make it home before dark?

Is there still a private place where a soul
can go and still find its own solitude;
to sit and gaze at the setting of your two brilliant suns?

Or is heaven so crowded with its teeming billions,
an entire ocean of dead humanity surging,
with no room to turn—souls everywhere

head to toe and toe to head,
all very speechless and
in absolute curiosity,
saying things like,

"I never knew it would be like this,
never in a million years?"

I turned to see a small robin,
red breasted with eyes leaping like fire,
she tilted her head as if to say,

"You really haven't got a clue, have you?"

That shadowy penumbra we know inside our soul—of our darker days and darker ways—well, it's been swallowed up by a light greater than you and I could ever imagine. Still, our stumbling and grasping natures continue to dominate and play the game, never knowing the copious beauty and the extravagant grace in which we are all engulfed.

| *PENUMBRA*

We are all probably
suffering from
an incredibly
chronic lack of awe.

| *LACK*

¶ SINGLE GLANCE

Illuminate yourself with a
single glance.

A burning eye full of
sight.

A body full of light.

Look at the inner
revolution taking place.

Each beat of your soul a
doorway to shining.

You and I have no idea
how wonderful it all is.

Illumina.
Illumina.
Illumina.

§ THIRST

A single drop of virgin beauty
for this terrifying world,
and all I need do is drink.

My thirst quenched
for a thousand years,
but by then, I also

will have fallen
into silence.

ꝗ IN THE GLADE OF THE FAE

Do you see that invisible door, it looks like
a swirl in a patch of fog or a flicker from a
moonbeam bright?

The distant is drawing near in strange and
beautiful visions of light.

My mind, tightly shut, was full of very grown-
up nonsense—brittle flowers, somberly
powdered in deathly white. Never wanting to
know what lay beyond the fragility of all my
shallow delights. I strangled mystery. I was
a sullen soul, trapped in the neon prisons of
what was regarded normal and correct. I too
fell in lockstep with the rest of our mortal race.

But this all changed, beginning late one night,
with the gentle swaying of the overhanging
branches of the old oak trees among which
I walked. A realm from silence and shadow
revealed itself, conveying ideas and wonder
from deep within their long green foliage that,
even now, I can scarce talk about without tears.

The sacredness of nature's wood lifted her veil.
A conspiracy of tranquility uncloaked itself
with utter abandon, unrolling forever a carpet
of beauty that has never known hate, but only
the soft breath of kindness and peace.

Deep within this tumbling forest lay the
memories of a once precious innocence. They
floated like glass boats on the glistening waters
of a still lake—a lake that was always so very
far away, yet now so very near.

"*Fly away with us and see, release the ground below and know*," came a sudden cry.

Tiny winged creatures of leaf and pure light, evidently lost to common sight, came from every direction to swarm around me—a swirling storm of tenderness mingling, like radiant butterflies or tulips with slender wings, of every hue from history's first dawn, so wide, so grand was this opening of evening light.

Deep delicate reds burned with intense beauty, the wild rush of orange and gold made sure my eyes remained half closed before them, tumbleweed and mountain meadow greens danced with dandelion air and a rich sun-glow yellow, and how could I forget the flowing wine of those wings ablaze in deep indigo and sky blue ice.

"*Down from the trees, down from the sky, up from the earth, over the lake's eye, following the wind, chasing the leaves, into the dark forest we fly.*"

The tempest of rainbows continued to rise—a continual flurry of wings and leaves and tiny faces. This rain of color and approaching beings could only bring me to my knees, and as the forest came alive with all manner of exquisite creatures, it was then their soft voices began calling again.

"*We know a place so very near, so very precious, so very dear, a distant world—so very clear, come, there is naught to fear from any shadow there.*"

Their invitations rang sweet, my desire grew strong. I was lost in a world so enormous that the great farce of my humanity (at least the humanity that I had come to know) came to a solid and abrupt end.

"Foolish man," I said to myself.

"I don't belong here."

I started to cry, yet the lightning of joy soon became my only song.

These sunset fountains, small and sparkling in the moonlight, poured out their life before me, profusely verdured in mirth and sweetness. Joy and serenity seemed to be their single view as the air about me began to shine like silver silk.

In this emerald glade, with its glassy waters of innocence forgotten, I had become a child again. The possibilities of life were reborn in the gathering of hundreds of nature's long hidden beings.

I could not help but wonder if they were all astonished at my countenance, as I was of theirs.

That night the wisdom of the forest shone, as if galaxies were split open and poured out a hidden radiance from overflowing golden cups. Again I trembled at this thought, as an uncreated, formless wonder, seized my heart the second time.

The forest now filled with flames of white light. "The wonders of the mind are bright this night—so very bright *this* night," I whispered to myself, still overpowered by fear mingled with delight.

"Come beyond the moon, beyond the night; come beyond the rivers and mountains high, only come..."

The waters of the lake were laughing now. The earth beneath my feet somehow released its ancient grip. The stubborn will of gravity gave way to a gentle sound of a single distant melody, what I can only describe as a hauntingly beautiful wooden flute.

I saw I was no longer earth-bound, something had engulfed my darkness, weight was no more, my very existence became a revery. Something had separated me from what I was before, and I shall never return the same.

Why was the sun so bright this night? Why do my eyes now shed tears? And why this faint quiver of remorse and fear in the face of beauty?

"Owls that speak, trees that sing, rocks that laugh, and leaves that bow before the ripple of ancient winds. You have no need to fear, no need for shame, for we have long been watching you and surely know your wonderful name."

With my feet hovering above the ground, I cried, "Have I died?

Have I departed to some eternal garden bright?

Shall I now forever remain voiceless to the common world of man?

Have I left my loved ones dear without ever saying a word?

Are they doomed to rehearse the countless questions of their loss? Will they ever know the wonders that now appear before me?"

Floating out of the light came a tiny face, dazzling white. Flickers of deep blue and wild green seemed to travel from beneath her feet all the way to edges of her flowing auburn hair.

Was it the influence of lingering moonbeams? A phantasm of a mind now on fire? A fever of madness, or night-dreams, or both?

Slowly she glides, as would a falling leaf adrift on a gentle spring breeze.

"Ah, you believe nothing the first time, do you?" she laughed.

Her voice was musical, soft, almost a murmur, like the rustle of a gentle wind amidst the leaves of a great tree, but very clear, and so very freeing. I let her talk on.

"I am a guardian of your memories, innocent and free. I have no shadow of which you can see. I float through your winter of soul and swallow the cold and darkness whole. All your gloomy beliefs I turn, all your blackest shades I burn."

She touched my tears with the tip of her pale finger, they immediately froze and fell to the earth, an icicle of unbelief shattering in a sudden burst of crystal blue light. I could have sworn the mossy roots of the trees let out a long sigh at each breaking.

Her tiny face again pondered my eyes as if she were looking right into the cave of my soul; into all those darker nooks and crannies I did not even know or want known, and with every graceful move of her wings a tint of what appeared to be blue fire rippled across her soft cheeks.

Scores of other creatures, just like her, still played and danced in the moonlight. These little angels (if they can be named such) were, of course, aware of my utter wonder, yet choose to yield their own desire and curiosity to the one who was before me now.

My heart was aflame, my mind reeling, my soul shaking, my strength exhausted—yet here I was, with neither fame nor fortune to call my own, nothing to boast of why I was granted such an audience.

I was afloat with hope (and still no small amount of fear—but not of the crippling variety, but of the awe one might gather before such immense beauty and wonder) and hearing her voice I became as wax before her words.

Under the gentle gaze of a moon, which now seemed closer than ever, I was being moulded and shaped anew. A chisel of light, a velvet hammer of love, a blade of compassion, and the breath of real magic.

My entire being lay open: vulnerable, naked, alone, but somehow beautifully belonging to this other world, a world far greater than my old universe of scientific fact and analytical data, of text book precision and bony truth.

That world can be cruel, crucifying all imagination, wonder, and the mystery of love.

"We are lined with lace and the triumph of grace; the caverns of your soul will now unroll, the wine of love will descend as a dove. Disguised in humanity is a divine rarity. Waters seethe and trees may bleed, but know the blood of the Fae is in you too. Our nectar is for you to drink, the rain of our tears, your eternal ring."

Long did I ponder her final gush of words as the low swell of horizon's coming dawn came all too quickly. I was barely able to walk home, and yet, in the fresh morning air, it was as if I was new-born.

My heart slowly returned to earth over the weeks that followed, though an ache within always made me return to the place that had changed my entire world.

As I recount the strange events that had befallen me that night, it seems they are shrouded in an eternal mystery, at times too intimate to talk about, too sacred to boast before adoring crowds who would pay well for such stories.

As such they remained silent for the last thirty years or so, until I felt a quiet voice say in my heart that now it is time to share of this long-hidden world.

Today, on hearing this tale, people often ask, "Is there a way to this forest? Is there a way to the *Glade of the Fae?*"

I can only reply with a sigh as I look at them straight in the eyes.

"I suppose there is," I say, "if one could find the way. It's both a precious and severe haven that'll rearrange your entire world. But be prepared, and look up, for under the full light of a twilight moon you may just hear a rustle in the leaves of the great oak trees and catch a glimpse of tender burning wings."

❡ THE GIRL WITH WILDFLOWERS IN HER HAIR

I followed the girl with the shimmering snow-white hair. The unnatural light around her flowed like a luminous mist, dissolving and curling around her lower legs and feet. Drawn towards her by an attraction as irresistible as it was incomprehensible, I was overcome before such purity and beauty. She took my hand and looked into the wide wells of my eyes, her voice streamed fluent as her many waters washed over me.

Her face was all aglow, yet translucent with a deep blue-green fiery swirl. She was gently swaying, bending as if caught in the caress of a small breeze. Nor could I say she was even standing upon the path before me, it was more that she glided upon a small pillow of air or water that kept folding in upon itself. She was but only a few inches higher over the ground where we stood.

"Trust the Oak," said she,

"you can always trust the Oak

with its deep roots and

giant welcoming arms,

and the Ash,

and the towering Elm,

for they all speak plainly."

"But the wild flowers,
it is they that are more prone
to utter mystery and enigmas
of speech, to them you have need
to pay close attention."

"They whisper in the
language of color and
breathe the tremors of light,
they sing sonnets of love and
know the reckless abandon of the wild.
Wildflowers delight to grow in
little clusters of mountain
or meadow freedom, where
the ever verdant and playful sylphs
mischief-make as they fly over their tiny
blushing faces."

"They do not care if you
love them or hate them,
pluck them or crush them,
believe in them or despise them,
their beauty is free,
their fragrance ever generous,
to devils as black as night,
to angels as white as light,
they do not judge who is

before them, of who is
worthy of their sight."

"If you step on such a creature's
slender home of beauty,
their tiny body and delicate soul
will shine, alas, no more,
their lifeblood will quickly wither
and turn to a final and solitary
sweet scent that is meant
to astonish and bless
even the hardest of souls."

I stood astounded at her words.
"Then it is no longer a flower
that I see," said I, "but a wave of
magic and mercy growing
upon every field and hill."

"The flowers are wisdom's true prophets,"
said she.

"Your seers and sages from all ages
have longed to see beyond the
heavy waves of night the engulf the heart,
of this violence that
shakes the soul of the earth,

of the hate that cannot abate,

of all the dark dreams aching for

some final release."

"Look," said she, pointing to a small hollow in
the woods.

There, a short distance ahead of us, a deer was
grazing, alone in her grassy bed of slumbering
meadow.

"Even she knows the thin crust of earth

on which she rests is full of living magic,

deep with the long memories of time.

She knows what great longing

lies upon these heavy tomes of land,

with its giant curling pages of green,

its drifts of fragrant pines and needles,

the scattered beds of spiraling leaves

and trickling streams.

So she treads gently, kindly, knowing the

forest also waits in shadows,

the ground itself crying out for release,

she too is desperate for the

birth of a wildflower light."

Something shifted,

something moved,

something shook loose in me.

I never knew the untouched wild would
expose my frippery and stun my wearied soul.
Her words were a salve sent from a universe I
had no idea existed.

Her presence was a flame to light the very
stars that were birthing within my own heart.
And all those haphazard slaps of shadow and
sunlight tiling a patchwork across this old
forest floor—here was a deeper, more ancient
light beyond light. Something seemed to come
alive within my soul that very hour.

❡ THE MADMAN

The old man was driven mad.

"Yes, quiet insane is he," some would say in hushed tones.

"His mind is unusually unstable," said others in a slow tongue and despondent look. "Why such a great and ominous cloud has appeared on this once brilliant and wonderful mind we shall never understand?"

No one could convince him otherwise that his absurd beliefs, his godlike indolence, and his equally proud spirit had bequeathed on him a dark and despised stiffness, and as such, this could be seen in his now grey and slave like countenance that was once so very gentle and kind.

I asked of the exact nature of this poor soul's horrid madness to those given charge of attending to his daily care, their reply came swiftly with an open air of grief,

"He hates us and does not believe we even exist; that none of our kind are real, that we are all mere phantasms and visitations of delusion which have no place on a sane and logical earth. The architecture of his darkness seems to know no bounds, nor do his frequent outbursts of obscene speech and violent gestures towards us abate in the least, some of us even fear for our very safety at times, but still, compassion compels us to not give up on this man, not yet anyway, but I fear it is worse

now than when this trouble first appeared
some months ago. Every night he seems to
sleep with savage beasts of a tormenting
kind, and upon waking becomes more self-
infatuated with his torrents of vanity and mock
self-control."

Before departing, the one who was speaking
to me turned and began to glow with an
immanent and bright fire, saying,

*"We are only lighthouses, forever burning over
broken and turbulent waters. We shall not allow
him to become choked by this quenchless sea
and be forever stranded upon a rocky shore of
mind."*

The wealth of her final words meant a strange
and warm comfort possessed my soul with
an intimate beauty. A kinder knowledge rose
up, one that meant the grey mantle of forlorn
hope would soon be cast aside for such a pitied
soul—his restoration would surely come.

And with that the gentle faced Faerie flew
off at the speed of light, along with several of
her companions, their small beating wings
shining as a beacon of hope against the
staring blackness of this man's constant eye of
disbelief.

¶ PHOENIX POSTMORTEM

Can I move at dream speed
to be where I cannot be,
to catch the true face of my soul—
not the actor, the painted stain,
the one without feet or voice
on display to this compulsive world?

I want to catch the eye of the flame of life
that hides behind the stone cold mountain
of my pulseless shadows and decaying
metaphors,
the space that is above,
below, beyond, within,
(or is it between)
what is and
what is not yet.

The simplest of things so often elude me,
like the 30 gallons of moonlight spilling
all over my desk and right up into my unsure
heart.

Somnambulist soul, why do you walk so slow?

Unlock the little cage of your vast circus of
illusion.

Run free from this duality and darkness,
they have become a sea at night
in which I sink with a brutal elegance.
Ditto to separation and senseless sight,
your small stunning-chains shadow me
with their heroin vision, fast and fluid.

There is a difference forever in the skylight,
sudden and violent and deepening.
I become rich when I disappear,
so I bid farewell to all that I am—
for all that I am I offer at the altar of love.

I will be rebirthed as a wobbly-legged phoenix
with tiny burning wings all a flurry,
but first I will sit and learn
to listen all over again.

❡ THE WELL AT THE END
OF THE WORLD

a prose poem

I imagine we cannot force our way into *the well at the end of the world*, to learn its infinite secrets, to bathe in its magical oils, or taste its golden delicacies. And to slide down its slippery silver sides and tumble in with a solid and illustrious plop will no doubt startle all concerned. If you are unprepared you will raise no small quarrel within your own heart, and even with time itself.

The well at the end of the world is guarded by tiny creatures with very bright faces and burning wings. Their small and fragile hands carry sharp thunderclaps and a swirl of deep blue storms clouds appears around their necks.

Their eyes are all ablaze in what can only be described as a dance of ruby flame, this seems, of course, to match their equally intoxicating song that fills the air with a tender and fragrant joy.

At *the well at the end of the world* you have to slow down, no, I mean you will really have to slow down. If you are too fast you will miss its azure surface and the ever tranquil mossy stones. Directly above you will see the swirling of hitherto unknown constellations, each inhaling the earth's far and distant memories.

And remember to pay close attention to the wondrous play of the creatures from countless worlds—they know their season is about to begin, and the very stars have all gathered for this special occasion.

Don't be surprised if you see the odd giant teardrop hanging precariously on the edge of the gracious sun of the night. Be not afraid, for at *the well at the end of the world* the moon cannot contain her feelings any longer. Each day she must release, without fail, the tremendous sighs of Gaia's everlasting song of love. If she held it in, knowing the immensity of the magic, she would be overcome and be quiet unable to function for several days.

Your great mind and chugging locomotive of logic and reason, heavy-laden with bundles of neatly packaged thoughts, must be left at the pools edge.

The tiny creatures with very bright faces say it will only turn your soul's wings to lead. "The well is very deep," they cry, "and stretches everywhere at once. And you don't sink down; oh no, no, you always sink upwards and outwards, far into the vastness of the Other Land. And it is deeper than you realize, deeper than the deepest valley that your immense soul can fathom, but some of you never listen, always spoiling the mystery because of your intellectual greed."

At *the well at the end of the world* you will prefer the madness of faery lore and magic, the light of the invisible world will ignite all around you.

It will make your child-like eyes flash in long forgotten wonder.

Tales of splendor and silence and music and wild beauty will fly straight into your open face. They shall come with the force of wind and rain, just ask the circle of tall oak trees when you are there—they understand best how to tell you of the new world that draws so near.

Often you will hear a gathering storm at the well at the end of the world, this can last longer than expected, sometimes a few days. A deep tremble of thunder, a roaring sea, a quaking land; the Old World is passing and the Other Land is coming to sweep you away to an ancient bliss.

Like waves it will hit you—ah, but first, the shiver of twilight, the slumber of darkness, an unfathomable sadness, the gathering storm. Then the chains of sorrow will snap like a twig and a great light will unhide all that you are, your entire countenance will sparkle with the very elements that gave birth to the universe.

Widespread over the human family a hand of iron fate and gloom broods beast-like. Violence and unending sorrow; the claws spread, but the color of heartache and sorrow is unknown at *the well at the end of the world.*

All races will be adored, all creatures (seen and unseen) will be cherished, all those imprisoned beneath earth and mountain and the ocean's dusky abyss will be released.

Scores of majestic winged beings will write upon the sky with golden rain. A thick white light will cluster around them like the nectar of the sacred berries from the Pegasus tree.

Before you step into *the well at the end of the world* you will be given a sapphire crown and a long flowing robe that looks more like a mantle of rainbow fog. Ceaseless it swirls and swims in the air about you that not a single thread of the fabric will remain still—this you shall adorn, like a glorious race of gods and goddesses newly enthroned.

A sublime wine shall be in your cup, a vast and sacred company your unending joy, a thousand-fold flame of life will engulf all who step into the well, for as soon as you take that step the Old World, even now with its mourning night and seething day, begins to decline.

You and I are possessed by a very great yearning, whether we realize it or not. It is to go and find that place, within or without us (we sometimes cannot tell) where the vast cathedrals of forest and soul tower above our intellect, where we can be cradled in a love that knows no boundaries.

| *YEARNING*

Ignorance always declares that I am a something; awareness will declare that I am actually nothing; love will declare that I am everything, for love eternally abides in the soul, and love always decreases the I and increases the divine.

| *Ignorance*

¶ ANGELARIUM

She fumbled in her bag for an umbrella,

one that was big enough to stop

the unrelenting downpour splashing

all around her feet—or was it an outpour?

Everything was soaked through and through—

her clothes, her skin, her bones, her soul,

the pavement, the street, the city,

the adoring earth, even the deepest oceans were

beginning to cry out, 'Enough! Enough!'

She was finally seminared out,

her conference batteries fully depleted, and

her meeting motivations wobbled on a thin trip wire.

She'd seen too many with the slick hair,

the cute faces, the trendy tunes, the rehearsed rhetoric,

the clichéd quotes dripping

with oodles of theoretical spirituality,

and all those hollow smiles that kept grinning

through a smirking fog that desperately tried to

look like enlightenment or love, but was not.

So she was on vacation, for the next decade if needed,

from techno-spirituality, the insta-bliss of

gee-wiz wisdom, and the circus of trumpets

puffing out bread-crust tunes of soul-devastation.

Yet here she was, with a soul many miles deep,
ascending the highest mountain in a moment,
entering the longing forest in a heartbeat.
She had split the wood and lifted a stone
and found only the wondrous beauty
of an intimate presence.

Her poetry glistened for the first time ever.
In the breathless beauty of the angelarium
the Seraphim lay bleeding, wounded by love,
drowning in the myrrh of her words.

She, a river of divine wisdom?

She, a sparkle and spiral of pure joy?

She, becoming one, forever aflame?

"Oh come—come watch her burn,"
the Seraphim cry, "come and see the wind
and the rain, untamed and wild, flow with
the deepest strength of moonlight."

¶ ILLUMINA

Illumina in the autumn
shade of the soul.

Oh cold wave, here I ache
to be without fear, forever,
without end.

Illumina in the trembling
face of white winter.

Oh dark earth, here I
long to be loved, forever,
without end.

Illumina in the luxury of a
deep-dyed spring.

Oh flowing air, here I give
up the need to be right,
forever, without end.

Illumina in union with
the affectionate summer
flame.

Oh pure fire, here I fall
deeper into the sun,
forever, without end.

ꝑ CANTO UNIO MYSTICA
(SONGS OF MYSTIC UNION)

> *"...in girum imus nocte et consumimur igni..."*
> *("...we circle the night and are consumed by fire...")*
> - The Bard of Sacred Leaves -

ONE: THE INVITATION

It was a remarkable invitation,

measureless in wisdom,

freeing my earth-clinging memories to

encompass the very center of my being.

"Oh delicate dryad, hiding in

your arbor bright—your voice the

sound of a star in full song, how you have gripped

my future with an overwhelming longing,

providing my pen with rich

tears to fill every empty page."

She, a master in her own right,

breathless in her purity,

energetic in her flame,

fluid in speech and melody; yet infused

with an irrepressible love that I could

not mistake. Oh, and yes, controversial,

certainly controversial,

especially the way she was not meant to exist.

She crept from the branches opening wide

my tangle of fears, exposing my deep

psychic wounds of misguided belief.

Though she moved like delicate snow

this was no children's game, when,

again and again, with

vehement clarity and

ruthless abandon, her small frame

and soft voice became a diamond heel

crushing my dark snake within.

TWO: THE FORBIDDEN PLACE

She, a crystal sun, a bud and blossom

on the sky tree of my heart.

Her aerial abode, alone and almost invisible,

a solitude on high among the secluded mists

of the tallest of pines. From there

her light poured into my cup

bringing me to the eye of the needle,

the pithy core of a long-missing wisdom

so widely unacknowledged

in the contemporary scene.

Having heard my lightest of footsteps

through the forest that fateful day she

descended and sat on a low hanging branch,

her faint wings shimmering out ripples of

night green and sky blue light,

"Almost a forbidden place," she mused, smiling.

She spoke of that which moved her heart

entreating me

to see as the forest sees,

to hear as the wind hears,

to know as all mystery knows,

to hush and listen to the slumbering

earth beneath and the

drifting clouds above.

Immediately I felt haunted and

slightly unstable—had I

crossed the boundary of

some earth-born god, did I happenstance

enter a sacred domain where

primeval trees and rocks and rivers

share some ruby-cup of forbidden sunlight?

Should mortal eyes even behold such things

from the winepress of creation?

THREE: GO GENTLY, GO DEEPLY

For a moment all was quiet—all was silent,
save my pounding heart writhing
in a sea of tormenting questions.
Her soft voice, petals on the wind, continued,
"Go gently, go deeply, go humbly…
become thoroughly persuaded of the
ocean of fire at the center of your being.
Comfort the broken of heart from
this, your tree of life, though still
a child in your being."

Her voice a mix of light and thunder, a consuming
majesty breathing its own sacred flame;
sweet and bountiful and immortal and
yes, absolutely terrifying.
My adult world began to close in around me -
I had never pondered a dryadic mantra, nor was I
about to start, but with my imagination captured
and a rare beauty burning I found myself
silently repeating her solemn words,
"Go gently, go deeply, go humbly…"

At first I wanted to run,
to rebel to the safety of reason and logic,
"Trees cannot speak! You are not real!"

My tone an uncomfortable mix of disbelief,

terror, and unbidden humor.

"Call me not wise for I fear I am

deaf to your burning words," I cried,

clinging to a nearby branch.

Unguarded, her voice rose again,

"Wayfarer, my words are not long

nor are they intricate,

they are simple and free, yet the

weight of aeons compels me to speak.

I only wish to leave you a legacy

of divine compassion and

for you to apprehend the

astonishing light that bears you close

since the very beginning

of your life."

She flew from branch to branch

wrapped in a pulse of green-fire light,

my already reeling mind could

only watch in wild wonder

at the thought of this chance encounter—

A dream? A trance? A blissful unveiling

of some enchanted portal?

FOUR: MYSTERIUM TREMENDUM

That afternoon the forest and this tiny creature
 became my *monastiques de mysterium tremendum,*
a breathing cathedral of wood and earth and leaf.
A hidden tranquility erupted
narrowing all my future choices.
With my defenses exceedingly breached,
my former world
descended into a glorious naught—she
had given me the forest as never before.

"Go gently, go deeply, go humbly…"
My soul remembered my name,
the one I was given before I was born.
With each faltering breath I trembled,
the snake has shed its skin and can now freely
dance toward the sky—a worm to an angel.

Dew-stars glistened in her hair,
her branch-like arms carried a verdant glow
as she nestled deeper into her ancient wood;
Who was I to be speaking with the
guardian of flowers and dreams
and of things unseen, infant leaves
became her shield and cloak; the mists
of twilight her train and splendor; the wisdom

of an nobler age her outpoured cup of grace.

Then came her final words,
"Your cry is awakening the earth,
your aching heart brings you
to experience every blade of grass upon
every mountain and valley with
the infinity of taste. The sky opens,
the wind runs wild, and you
feel it all as Sophia's sweet river surges
in your lightning soul.
Beauty shall rise in the east
and unveil her holy face,
your garden will be in ever-bloom,
from snow drift mountains to the
roaring of the eastern seas; so shall beauty
sneak past your defenses, lean over
this dark earth and find a place
of enchanted rest."

With the final beating of her wings
the earth trembled beneath my feet and
the sky above blushed a soft whisper
of crimson as her autumn-full
hair caught the fading light, a glimmer
of dew-drops gathered upon her cheeks
as a selfless beauty shone from her eyes.

I fell to my knees
dripping wet with wonder.
My soul encompassed by a fragrance
that filled the air with
hope and longing.
It was already night and a light rain
began to fall; and, falling it was rain,
but having fallen it became a
star-dust of green and gold.

The entire forest seemed to be singing,
undivided and one,
singular and timeless,
a boundless hymn,
a flooding stream, and
all I could do was weep
as I watched its flow.

Even to this very day
I remain undone;
alone with her words;
voiceless, yet full.
A leaf blown in a strong wind.
A green seed scattered to be
wounded among the
sphere of the earth.

❡ BEFORE THE BEAUTY OF WORDS

The words on the page were not new,
it was simply the way they fell together,

soaring freely across my field
an elegant flock of wild angels, singing, swooping
with their cheeky grins and bamboo flutes.

I cannot explain the effect they had on me,
a diamond enchantment shining in my mind,
a pure breeze drifting like fireflies in a dark wood.

Would I hug myself,
maybe even levitate
a few feet from the floor?

It was probably quantum.

I moved from cool to warm,
eyes closed, breathing deeply, rethinking.

I should roll the syllables in
my mouth just a little longer,
like tiny honey pebbles captured in the
gentle caress of a delectable stream.

So with hands trembling over the page

I await the next knife to cut

right through my adverbial gland

so I can roam their worded prairies and hills

as an unchained ghost in search of poetic bliss.

¶ PLEONASM (IN BLUE)

Here,
in the vastness of a small
poem, you can wade out
into the blue ocean,
sink slowly into the
deep sea of meaning,
linger long on the lost shores of
a tearful silver moon,
hoping to squeeze out that
rare elixir that will
turn your world into
paradise.

Wouldn't you,
if you could?

Pleonasm: The use of more words than are necessary to convey meaning.

¶ THE BRIEF PASSING OF A
POETIC THOUGHT

It grew at the edge of one of my deeper sighs, gathering a strange momentum as my curious mind responded to its increased vitality. This enchanted cup sparkled near the brim, overflowed, and lit a fire within. The odd thing is that this all happened within the space of several moments. The noiseless foot of time, this winged hour of soaring thought, had no regard for common chronography, and, setting its footprints deeper than one could have ever imagined, beckoned me to wander in the garden of angels. I was simply asked to reflect the light of the ten-thousand diamonds burning at the edge of their deep infinity pools:

The revealing of soul.

The breach of nature.

The weakening of power.

The echo of sanity.

The dew of memory.

The cathedral of life.

"I guess I am not as resilient
as I thought I was."

The seep of fog.

The dragon-born game.

The broken glass.

The shameful past.

The skyscraper walls.

The rules of the world.

"I am desperately trying
to make sense of my life."

The stirring of illusion.

The sage of enlightenment.

The depression of struggle.

The bludgeon of reality.

The compression of thought.

The literary word unveiled.

"What is it that stirs
this mortal frame?"

The expansive moment.

The cadence of feeling.

The impressions of soul.

The nectar of the forest.

The elevation of spirit.

The art of imagination.

"Why has such beauty lie
down before me?"

The glimmer of intelligence.

The enchantment of flowers.

The awakening of consciousness.

The abundance of the eye.

The poverty of language.

The garland of mystery.

"Can my thoughts ever be
clothed in words that flame?"

The nature of serenity.

The chalice of beauty.

The conquering of love.

The wound of death.

The breast of angels.

The unfathomable mystery.

"I shall blush with wide-eyed delight at
the infinite riches of this little room."

The breath of a divine flute.

The feast of jewels.

The myriads of thought.

The undreamed shores.

The pale-faced moon.

The entrance of light.

"I think the slow moon has secrets still to
dust upon my roaming heart."

The halo upon us.

The hammer of gravity.

The flashes of a dying sun.

The rise of an emerald wave.

The speechless fields of radiance.

The reveling of moonlight.

"And all I want to do is stand silent,

your arms wrapped around my shivering soul."

⸾ WHAT THE BADGERS SAW

Here we are again,
another bewildering dialogue,
a brave nocturnal poem that may hold a
key to the great conundrum of your
fog-drenched reality. And all I

require of you, the reader, is to reach deep
into your exotic blue jeans and pull out
a small emotional investment in
the undertones of these obscure sentences
unsatisfied to remain alone.

Despite the singular reference to
'bright sunlight' or a 'swarming city' I prefer to
plunge you into the same atmosphere
of a deer as she stills her heart in the early mist,
her silver-skin shining, a corridor of breath rising,

the grass and meadow her golden carpet,
the thunder of silence lingering beside a small stream,
a silhouetted shape of grace in a vanishing world,
and the little badgers watch from a distance
beneath a shaded row of trees.

This poem is trying to
create silence with words;
a rare souvenir photo that can be
placed gently in your album of your soul.
And as you sit alone at night in

one of those cafes where a strong
north wind snaps across your face, I hope
you discover a little more than
your favorite punctuation marks
for this turbulent season of life.

¶ SURREALIST SERENITY

In the archive of the mind, a liquid flower blooms.

In the beat of the heart, the blueshift of grace.

In the tremor of the soul, a dancing fire weaves a pearl necklace.

In the empire of the will, a bottomless jade lagoon with floating stones.

In the forest of dreams, a cloud garden with burning tulips.

In the deep well of ego, the bumblebee of hope performs her slow dance with twilight-red ribbons.

In the trembling voice, the thunder of exploding paper tears.

In the lake of emotions, the transcendent color of a mauve reality.

In the library of memories, a moonlight hand turns the pages of all the books.

In the upturned face, the emollient bruises of a more heroic light.

In the kiss of expectation, a crystal forest perfumes the flight of migrating swans.

¶ WAR

And War,

drunk with oil

and might,

fell to earth laughing,

saying,

"Good morning,

I'm death,

I come in peace..."

My outer poet is arguing with my inner poet: "incoherent and hideous," "a thought crime," "as articulate as a houseplant," and on and on it goes...

| *This Writing Life*

¶ HIDING IN YOUR POCKET

God is in your typewriter, hiding under the letter G.

God is in your 2B pencil, tightly wrapped around that grey vein of magic clay. There is not much room in there, between the wood and the swirl, but he believes if he is still enough you probably will not notice.

God is hiding in your pocket, trying not to make a shuffling sound between the white pages of your spiral bound notebook. He likes to collect all your piled up letters and create beautiful poetry in a white-snow voice.

And do you see that tiny bubble floating to the top of that bottle of black ink? Yes, that's right, the one sitting on your candlelit desk before your open hearth. Well, God cannot hold his breath forever, can he—some things just give him away.

Candlelight perception has its own special finesse, a reverence appropriate to the flickering shadows of your soul. I guess God likes to hang out in the darkness also—though it does, at times, seem a little inappropriate for such a great being of pure light.

You can never tell if he is gently opening the dark caverns of your soul, exploring your uncharted inner world and offering you some fragile words for your next poem, just so you can begin to make sense of that ache you feel deep down inside.

Yeah, you know all about that—don't you.

That part of you hiding from the mystery of
who you really are; that part of you reserved
and hidden—well, why doesn't this somewhat
obscure and disguised deity just plonk himself
down on a chair right in front of me and have
a good old heart to heart?

Is he shy? Maybe he is afraid he won't be able
to answer a few questions that you wrote in
your notebook. I suspect he is still probably
trying to get his head around your biography
of darkness and wonder.

Maybe he also doesn't like the brilliant
white light and the frigid cold air of hospital
operating theaters—perhaps they send a shiver
up and down his divine spine and cause him to
blink a little harder.

He probably prefers to remain sneaky, quietly
weaving through the forest at night like some
holy mist, gently stirring the lucid shapes
of the green leaves and the great branches,
befriending shadows with a slow light and a
numinous nudge.

Maybe he is shy after all, not liking the things
that give him away with a loud voice and a
sharp aggressive light. He probably prefers
to be alone by himself sometimes, reading
Japanese haiku near some high mountain
waterfall. They tend to bypass the narcissistic
knots of those more wordy gushes in favor of
the liturgy of the simple.

Deep down, each one of us is a mystic for we all exist in the Mystery. We breathe her air; we drink his water; we long for a hope that eclipses our very souls in brightness. Whether we realize this or not is another thing altogether. But awakening to this, even if just one eyelid pops upon for a moment, will cause a grand reorganisation of one's entire universe.

| *MYSTICS*

The full moon of heartbreak comes all too often and all too soon to many a precious soul on this fragile earth.

| *HEARTBREAK*

Flowers have no mind, no thought, no great learning; yet they lure the butterfly. A butterfly has no mind, no thought, no great learning; yet visits the flower. When the flower blooms, the butterfly comes; when the butterfly comes, the flower blooms. Do you not see the ebb and flow of a gentle wisdom and harmony in life occurring beyond the realm of cold facts and empirical knowledge?

| *FLOWERS*

¶ THE DRYAD FROM THE
FOREST OF POEMS

A dryad fair from the *Forest of Poems* came to me late one night.

Her leaf wings were of indigo and sky-green, each bathed in a soft-snow light.

The evening moon joined in her song

Her words the breath of starlight strong.

"Draw ever near, have no fear, I have a message for you my seer," she began:

> *"I too want to transcend the trees, become seamless, fluid, air-like—a garment of momentary light, a distinctive voice with a debut song full of soul.*
>
> *I am a tiny dark horse dazzling, galloping beyond the fields of status quo to drink from the magical streams of the unexpected.*
>
> *I too am on a spiritual journey, breaking conventions to soar to outer worlds and inner realms. Beyond the forest glades, beyond the branches and leaves, beyond the earth, beyond all reach.*
>
> *The winnowing of my gorgeous nothings will fall like light rain upon a thirsty earth continually craving for more.*
>
> *That one great lake lies deep in my soul also, a swell of lyric and love, my distilled utterance paints an aching sea forever caressing a longing shore.*
>
> *Wade out with me into these waters, let them cradle us till distant suns toss their bouquets of light into our small embrace.*
>
> *But before letting me go, open yourself completely, still the petals of your mind and I will strike your bones with fire."*

She came very close to where I sat. That such a delicate creature could become so powerful in her embrace of word and song I could scarce believe what I was now witnessing.

"You should see your face right now."

She laughed out loud, mirth and joy filling her deep autumn eyes.

"From where have you come, and why me, why now?" I cried.

"I am gathered from the Conclave of Light, kind heart, kind soul," she smiled, face and indigo wings aglow. Then, as if struck by an immediate presence of such delight, a radiance so very bright shone at once from her tiny face. Her deep forest eyes became as bright as two white suns—she closed her lids and started to spin in a slow circular motion before me, becoming a tiny whirlpool of wings and air and hovering light. Time seemed to stand still as if trapped in some great vortex of expectation before this forest soul ascending. Slowly she circled around and around—slowly she rose, head arching back like a tightly stretched bow. All the time her wings beating in a wild and fearless rhythm that splashed little droplets of auburn light over my upturned face.

She opened again her mouth,

> *"What is this flame that is rising high in the night? What is this loving heart that draws so close in sight? I see all your sensitivity, your gentleness to the whole of realm of life, to all persons and creatures, to things seen and unseen—you are no stone hardening your face to any person or thing, I see a rare light deep in your soul."*

I began to cry, almost uncontrollably, yet she continued with the wind of her words almost oblivious to my trembling presence.

> *"I know you've seen the worst of the world, your heart has been broken and stoned many times, but I am giving you the heart of a poet. You have been waiting for the sun, some marvelous light to guide you in your blackest night, but I will be with you in your evening dreams, I am there to make you see.*

And when you dream of me you will see a distant shore flood in unbroken song. Willows will dance, rivers will shine, the great oaks will bow and become silent as you strike the harps of the evening stars lingering deep within your soul.

Darkness may fall around you, but your heart will remain true.

The black knives of fear may sharpen their shadowy blades.

Misunderstanding and spite the shade of night may draw near, but your face will remain calm and walk gently before their threatening gaze.

I shall make your words windows of light.

I shall make the sea your deepest ink.

I shall make the trees your pages of thunder and rain.

I shall make the stars your eternal communion of love.

You are not to shout,
or lash out,
to suffocate,
or dictate,
to conquer,
or smother another.

You are to expand and give voice to those that have none. You are to calm, to share, to lay bare, to reveal, to paint in colors the universe has never seen. To unleash a gentle space called destiny and quietly nudge souls closer to the love that they are absolutely terrified of, but are desperately hungry for.

I call you poet and my silence will sing long after I am gone. We belong to the same heart—of forest, of stream, and mountain's whispering.

You are storm and light, wind and humble might. Thunder cannot be muffled, but it can be harnessed to sound like a mighty flute pouring out a fragrant song across the earth and beyond.

I call you poet and I am simply inviting you to add your flame to the final gathering of infinities slow fire."

I'm not always so sure I want
to give myself over to spiritual
transformation. What will be
required? How will I change?
What will my friends and
family think? What new
dark night of the soul will I
have to endure? Will I lose
myself in the process? But
then again, *losing myself*
might be the very best thing
to happen—that fake, false-
self that sits on a brittle bone
throne. My journey through
deeper levels (if there is even
such a thing) of spiritual
growth is always voluntary.
I must continually consent
to Spirit. Transformation
is only this, always this—
over and over again.

|*TRANSFORMATION*

The rain fell—

just to touch you.

¶ THE SYMPHONIQUE SOUL

Ours is a symphonic journey of soul. We encounter light and darkness, self and God, truth and error, wisdom and folly, emotion and deadness, fear and bliss, struggle and rest. We all encounter our own perplexities as we come to grips with all that is infinite and divine, asking ourselves: what is our place within the great awakening that is marvellously touching so many of us?

I am coming to an abrupt stop.

I am trembling as a distant silhouette.

I am too drunk on words.

I am a soul of God in birth.

I am a million miles away from
        what I once was.

The heavy-laden wings of a soul entering light.

The holy, unspeakable, mysterious night.

The vast space bursting forth from
        inside to outside.

The depths of love that surge like an ocean.

The sky regions that are filled with
        a bliss ineffable.

It was a most unlikely place for
        a disappearance.

It was a painted mannequin life of
        regret and routine.

It was always 'off to sleep' with not even a clue.

It was starting to be 'I can almost see you'.
It was a sudden shattering embrace.

I am lost in a small war, so deadly, so vast.
I am now blind; so I can truly see—
    a poet from oblivion.
I am a beating heart; faster, faster,
    yet unusually still.
I am a gust of wind, a temple sage,
    an ember of grace.
I am overcome by the lost jewel
    of beauty divine.

The explanations were all missing.
The sun and moon finally collide in my chest.
The next wave of weeping poets are wandering.
The nocturne to the light of the stars.
The nectar is rushing inside my heart.

It was never enough.
It was a hard cold thaw.
It was bathed in awe.
It was pounding in reverence.
It was a final severance.

I am overcome by beauty divine.
I am speechless again, my lips are marble.
I am so frail before the cloudless deep.

I am in a daze before the sky-wind
  and wine-light.

I am a skeleton thrown down before
  unexplained wonder.

The explanations were all missing.

The terror of the ocean-world subsides.

The untold peace of silent mystery.

The uncertain depth of falling into sun.

The ancient blurring of two into one.

It was a longing that came into my heart.

It was tearing apart my emaciated way.

It was always a search for the clenched fist
  of a thousand reasons.

It was forever bowing before the tides of men
  and their towering minds.

It was the burning eloquence of another
  universe appearing.

¶ MOON BIOGRAPHY
MAGNIFIQUE

The old moon dangles

another snowdrop of quiet light—

a white sanctuary

hanging by a thread as it

floats cloud-like over

our frantic souls.

I was ignorant.

I was graced.

I was awakened.

I was consumed.

꧁ SATORI

Truth must be avoided at all costs.
I can't have hand grenades rolling
about inside my soul
unpinned.

Deep poetry is jugular, blood-red,
a velvet hammer and feather-white chisel
carving at a mountain of satori
just outside my view.

Exploding prismatic poem-light,
unmapped and unstunted delight,
saturate, astonish, enter the mind,
for you are not partial, but infinite.

Play a tune on your wild sand flute,
wishing away my life
of mistaken perceptions
that lapped at the surface of nothing.

¶ SEASHELLS

I walked along the beach this morning
joined by ten-thousand seashells, little
planets drifting across their morning light
universe, white jewel stars with
soft ripples of a lunar wave across their
terra nullius crust.

And I wondered if those far away tiny
sea creatures swimming in the moon's
Lacus Solitudinis; floating incognito
in their silver mink dust—
do they spy from afar and say,
"There he is, standing on
the sand again. There he is,
still scribbling in his little notebook?"

But they do not see:
at the center I am shaking
at the opulent and the invisible,
at the robed simplicity and the
blushing petals of solitudes light,
at the shore just beyond this one,
where the theatre of the spiritual
quietly writes on every seashell
something very delicate,
very shining, and very present.

Terra Nullius:
Nobody's Land

Lacus Solitudinis:
Lake of Solitude

ꟻ CAN SOULS DANCE
IN COLOR?

I want to color my soul
while biting into a pomegranate
on the hot dusty streets of Varanasi,
near the Ganges.

To look sideways
and nourish a different sight
as the cannons of
beauty and intensity
fire a riverside volley of
ordinary brilliance and
deep horrors across
my moving bow.

It's all a-swirl here,
a feverish intermingling,
ten-thousand hearts longing,
and I fear with each touch
of perfumed dirt I become
engaged with the gorgeous
world of words and promise,
all over again.

Let me crawl
inside my audacious clichés,
away from the stratosphere
of normal blindness that blows
little theories of everything
around my tired feet.

For I know I am prone to
entropy—my balanced
ecosystem and I;
and the worm of cosmic pessimism
sometimes squirms, and
like a mass of empty calories,
desires to be in my mouth.

Can I learn to breathe beyond
dying ash for oxygen?
It can be chaotic, vicious even,
but so exhaustingly beautiful
to find the personal
and the universal,
the soul's serenity resting in
a deep shimmering,
like soft moonlight
on some vast river.

There are no unsacred places;
there are only sacred places
and   desecrated   places—
including   your   own   soul.

| Sacred

¶ I WANT TO WEAR GOD

"At first, the best metaphors give you a rude shock,
then that deep smile of recognition."

Sometimes it seems as if our souls

are made of pulpy papier-mâché,

plastered all over with

nostalgia and green paint,

perhaps a fairy-tale elf hides in the

camouflage of some great concrete forest.

Souls can be squeezed into

a frigid piece of frost,

gentle, but alone,

and dreadfully prone

to the cold,

mimicking the colors of

white shadows upon stone.

What if they bleed unchecked

for a hundred years or more?

Desperate, scattered,

the loneliness of night's deep womb

forever bidding light farewell in

a dark-raven vein of sorrow.

Then, if they are purified by sorrow,

noble be that flame of

mysterious love which burns.

This birthing kiss

in which we flounder,

in which we flourish—

this grip of the terrible

and the tender, the heavy clouds

of a furious love with

mercy in her eyes.

"Be not sad, my beloved,

soon you shall see,

soon you will know,

soon this too will pass."

Perhaps at the center of the soul

lies the birthplace of

thunder and snow,

fire and rain;

creation's tears lamenting

for that which is truly wild and free.

Then can you ravish me till I see

beauty without misted eyes?

I think the soul would like to be

a vat of deep indigo wine,

fermented for a time such as this.

A glory conceived in winter, yet

set on fire by the stars.

A world living within you,

elusive and rich,

dignified and fearless,

vast, yet containing

a soft and beautiful shy

in rhythmic sway

with the universe.

Oh, and yes, always

grinning from ear to ear

because it knows it's

wearing God.

An old and wise man was sitting by a river when a young man interrupted him. "Master, I wish to become your disciple," asked the younger. "Why?" replied the old man. The young man thought for a moment. "Because I want to find God." The master jumped up, grabbed him by the scruff of his neck, dragged him into the river, and plunged his head under water. After holding him there for a minute, with him kicking and struggling to free himself, the master finally pulled him up out of the river. The young man coughed up water and gasped to get his breath. When he eventually quieted down, the master spoke. "Tell me, what did you want most of all when you were under water." "Air!" answered the young man. "Very well," said the master. "Go home and come back to me when you want God as much as you just wanted air."

| *AIR*

Once a *returning* takes place the cries of the great heart-poets are heard in the soul. Poetry from Hafiz or Rumi or Kabir or David in the Psalms, even many of the Romantic poets is open to new eyes. The soul longs for union with the Beloved as a wave returns and dissolves into the ocean, even though it is still remains wave. "I and the Father are one," said Jesus. And where the Christ lives, he also invites us to experience that oneness or union with God. And until we know this we are eternally restless in all our false separations. Until we know we are loved and that an infinite love indwells us, now, and forever more, we shall always be searching for love in externalities, but there is no love that can be found in the external for the Kingdom (Queendom) of God has always been within.

| *Union*

Walk barefoot upon this hallowed Earth, dance to its rhythmic heartbeat, bury your feet in the warmth of the soil, or the cool of the green grass, frolic in fields of flowers, crunch through leaves and skip along stones. But most importantly, feel yourself become whole.

HoneyCoyote (Tumblr)

¶ DEEP POETIC THROMBOSIS

I was told *this* thought was special,
that it had a poem trapped inside
its large black vein of smoky pathos,
and if not seen to immediately,
swelling would occur
because of the blockage.

The location and size of the poem
was yet to be discovered in detail,
but it is known that thoughts causing
such large poetic clots can face
complications and are best managed with
open heart surgical techniques
rather than poking around
at the mysterious lump of letters
now forming at the edge of my
blank page.

Recent tests included an
ultrasoul scan advising
that I sit by my window
for a far longer period of time
than previously expected,
placing a tiny needle in
the back of my head to allow

the aesthetic of another world
to take its desired effect.

I was further advised not to drive
for at least forty-eight hours
after the poem finished its final sulk
in the shadows of a lingering depression,
and to disregard such advice would
cause the moon in the upper corner
of my thoughts, to hang there stubbornly,
refusing to offer any ancient glow at all.

So there I sat—peering
over the empty page,
face to the glass like a
pigeon tap-tapping at the pane
wanting to come inside
and warm itself from cold. However,

I wanted to go outside
to where the soft blades of green grass
were admiring my determined looks,
and to talk to the tall forest oaks
beyond my little fence, whom I was told,
had perfected a circulatory kind of magic;
a weave and whoosh of sap and sunlight that
was sure to bring some relief
to the flow of muse still trapped within.

¶ BIOMAGICAL BEING

I am still amazed at
the hundred-trillion cells
in this vast colony of me,
humming away in organizing harmony,
all a part of this biomagical being I am,
inseparably connected and unique,
visible, yet unseen—
a soul wrapped in a fabulous skin
that carries tears a plenty at the
amazing rush of crimson-pink
from the fresh oven of a creeping dawn.

And that great cosmic stork,
the one with such inconceivable light
bursting from each wash of his wings,
he carried this tiny pearl of me
across the river of
such breathtaking space.

And despite my nervous laughter that
often believes his swirling compass must
have become very lost as he glided
past the outer rings of Saturn,
it seems his celestial route to earth
was met with grand applause and
that he didn't drop me off at the
wrong end of the universe after all.

Please kiss me awake.

I need to stop hurting.

¶ POETRY FOR THE BITTER HOUR

This is not a poem

with soft pink lips, perfume sweet.

Nor is it a bursting sonnet

seeking love in the flower fields of forever.

And I don't think it's a

spiritual rap with staccato stanzas

shackled and tangled in the wild wind.

Maybe it's the dirge of a holy believer

counter-claiming truth and beauty

in hope of the glory of money,

or possibly a

Zen snapshot haiku:

'cherry blossom wisdom full

the river surges.'

Ah, but then, no, I think it might be a

small smile of lullabies

long imprisoned in my skin,

now sitting and waiting to be

sung gently awake during the bitter hours

of some great future apocalypse.

¶ POETRY DOESN'T HAVE TO RHYME

Poetry doesn't have to rhyme, it just has to
clatter down the cobblestones of your cold
and lonely thoughts with its blazing torch held
tight.

Poetry doesn't have to rhyme, it just has to
leave you shaking in its light, naked and
exposed in its pure breath.

Poetry doesn't have to rhyme, it just has to
move with hushed voice and quiet footsteps
right into your heart's most secret place.

Poetry doesn't have to rhyme, it just has to
pour from the sky and blow across your dark
moors, drenching all your deep ravines with
an ocean of tears.

Poetry doesn't have to rhyme, it just has to
leave a loaded gun full of half-cocked word-
triggers trembling in your soul.

Poetry doesn't have to rhyme, it just has to
open those trapdoors hidden beneath our skin,
giving our hearts an ever-so slight nudge with
its shocking beauty.

Poetry doesn't have to rhyme, it just has to
wipe away those mascara-stained tears now
stitching a dark trace across your pure cheeks.

Poetry doesn't have to rhyme, it just has to
steal your eyes far far away to another world,
another time, another dream, another mind—

holding you still till you either smile or weep, or both.

Poetry doesn't have to rhyme, it just has to prove to you that he is a rebel sorcerer, the greatest wielder of magic alive, beaming from ear to ear with a silk grin and a holding a wand made from whispers and paper stars.

Poetry doesn't have to rhyme, it just has to promise you azure dreams and rainbow pearls, sights that sooth the loss of a thousand lesser woes groaning in the dark halls of your mind's more desperate days.

Poetry doesn't have to rhyme, it just has to woo like Dante's high speech tumbling from a high heaven or a hateful hell. Flocks of angels and storms of devils move wordlessly, laugh, and blink as you open again to their rare and unseen magic.

❡ YOUR STREETS ARE NO
LONGER GOLDEN

Written as my mind reeled from the devastating earthquake that hit
Kathmandu and the surrounding regions on 28th April, 2015. Now
known as the Gorkha earthquake, it killed over 8,000 people and
injured more than 21,000. I have traveled and spoken in Nepal several
times.

Lately I've found I

just stare at the tangle of

stars above me

as they carry me home

from another earth aching.

I'm barely breathing.

"Another dead baby."

My desperate poetry praying.

"Another dead mother."

Your streets are no longer golden,

your sights and sounds departed,

the fragrance of dead things

dulls the air.

"Another fresh-born specter glides past."

Certain things dry out the soul

and clog the tears.

Thousands of your dead

gather in shrouded huddles,

watching, still trembling

as soft stones tumble their gentle skin.

There is death in the clouds:

the sky pours down tombs—

another kiss, the shade of gravity.

Into the light of the dawn

they wander like jewels unformed

fighting to hold back the tears

of those they left behind.

I gaze upon the grey grey scenes of

the year they lost April.

I want to switch off the light for a while

just to sit in the darkness,

alone with my hidden world of questions

that will never get answers.

I think there's a hole in the sky.

Is that a dirty halo above me,

staring at me, watching me from afar

through the light of my window?

And lately I've found I

desperately want to sing

with the stars

as they carry me home

from another earth aching.

¶ *THE GREAT WAR OF*
  INFINITY

Beat the poets of infinity into silence if you must. Feed us shifting sands
till wonder disappears from off the earth. Bind us in vulgar chains of
fetid logic and reason till tears flow and fill every grave afresh with grey.

But we shall rise with marvelous eyes, wearing silken crowns fit for a
thousand queens. Burning quills with serene blue sight, and a diamond
chalice overflowing with remarkable unwritten epiphanies.

We shall burn across Orion's long night sky—on white dreams our
brave soul-birds will stretch wide their noble wings of brilliant light.

We all remember the babble, tinker, and gush of that single under
water moment when the flood of love overturned every stone of mortal
consciousness. Ever since then we swim with emerald mermaids
robbed in the crystal pearls of a greater deep.

We are not a civil wood nor a well trimmed hedge, but a wild forest
incubating unseen beauty—a swan light, sky bright, banishing the
darkest night.

The glory of angels, the dross of jesters, the blades of wizards, the
angst of gods lesser, the tears of rage, the bliss of dreams, the shyness
of dying stars, the illusions of blinded eyes—all these rhymes of mystic
splendor—they cannot rest their burning legends in the rusty relics of a
passionless prison.

So brag if you must, of your unfailing reason, strain at gnats and write
your poison. Enthrone your mind and choke all secrets, whisper in
shadows and drain the lake of meaning, but know the poets of infinity
will live again under the rising dawn of a holy anarchy.

I often wonder if you go off into
a far, far forest and become
very, very quiet, will you come
to understand that you're
connected with everything?
Will you come face to face with
your fears, your hopes, your
dreams, your *real* identity,
your ravished heart beating
for a deeper connection
with the God particle and
everything else? I wonder if
that green prophet of creation
will reduce the tension tearing
at your mind? Will the silence
of the trees be whispering
louder than ever before?

| *SILENCE OF THE TREES*

By hating another, you
lose something very
precious within yourself.

| *HATE*

The mystical nature of one's belief is a very
well-kept secret. It does not serve the interests
of empire, or patriarchy, or churchiness,
or cult, or trendy spiritual movements, or
religion's entrapments, especially the elite
guards who think they are breathing the
rarified air of such unconquerable orthodoxy.
It is coming alive again, in your very soul,
for their lies the essence. You are hearing the
voices of the mystics and the prophets of all
the ages. Your deepening of this awareness is
an underground river about to burst its banks.

| *The Secret*

True mysticism is among the finest of gifts that
your soul can know, for mysticism is about
that subtle mix of awe and gratitude; it is about
letting go to all that is, and then letting be.
It is about birthing new life, about releasing
all that pent-up creativity inside, and about
compassion—a compassion that brings healing
to our planet and inviting the millions of souls
walking about its groaning surface to drink
sunlight.

| *THE SUBTLE MIX*

I'll show you the wonders of Wonderland, and
when you're drunk on the beauty and chaos
that your heart so yearns to know, I will take
you under my wings and make you forget the
human realm ever existed. You'll never want to
leave Wonderland or me again.
- A. G. Howard

| *WONDERLAND I*

Sometimes spiritual transition hurts. You will struggle with all you have once believed and held precious. At times you will hear Alice whisper, *"I almost wish I hadn't gone down that rabbit-hole—and yet—and yet—it's rather curious, you know, this sort of life!"* Sometimes a flame must turn an old forest of dry wood to ash before the seedlings burst through the scorched surface—then new growth can begin. I believe our former Wonderlands, once very pristine and correct, need a thorough burning to cull dead belief and resurrect the new. You know you can't turn back the clock to the common way of seeing things, you can only move forward, stumbling from one bright light to another, one level of glory to another, one level of seeing to another (until even the whole concept of 'levels' or 'glory' themselves seem to lie dead in the water). For then you will glimpse only one vast ocean of love swallowing up everything in its own pevading beauty.

| *Wonderland II*

¶ THE ANGELS OF THE NINTH
   DAY

"Oh?" the curious crowd would say.

"Do tell…do tell us more of the angels."

"Oh," said I, "they doze twenty-five hours a day,

eight days a week, then, on the ninth day

they slip into the fantastic oceans of space

and come to the worlds that are deeper down

carrying phosphorescent leaves, green and glowing."

"Oh why…tell us why do they carry the leaves?"

"Oh," said I, "the leaves are from the Garden of God,

they grow on lightening trees and are plucked by the

enormous *white-wings* for the stilling of violent cities.

The *white-wings* sing the songs of the infinity-stars and are

so very gentle with the healing leaves, packing each one

in a moonlit ocean jar, carefully mixing it with light and peace.

"Oh my…tell us more of the *white-wings* and of their songs?"

"Oh," said I, "the *white-wings* are the holy Pegasus doves

with long memories of Dark Eden's savage rape of the earth,

their cloud-born poetry has spoken of this for countless moons,

they know of the ancient collisions of magic,

they know how it seduces and fights for the

consciousness of the human race, but the leaves they carry

reverse this ancient forest's violent glow."

"But why…why are our cities so very violent?"
"Oh," said I, "look, do you not see all those chimneys,
look at the long puffs of snoring filling the sky. Look
above their heads, do you see all those unlit clouds? Do you
see the thick splashes of sewery grey tumbling about the earth,
covering everyone's shadowed feet?"

"Do tell…tell us why they are so cruel and violent?"
"Oh," said I, "beasts do feed on what they breathe,
wet and heavy things creep in unseen, slithering
like illusions into their very souls—the forsaken
dregs, the dribbles of darkness, the black opiates of the soul,
the brooding grimness from the aftershocks of time,
the unseeing sight of ancient world echoes.
This… this is why we need the angels of the ninth day."

"But when… when shall these angels again appear?"
"Oh," said I, "they have been here since time began,
yet so few have believed, so how could they see;
and if they have never seen, how could they ever
eat from the bottled lightening leaves?
But time itself conspires against darkness in a beautiful way.
Hopes abides, even within as a tiny blush of light,
resting upon each one's weary sight. Prophecy and
fantasy are becoming one in the immortal days ahead,
and we shall all be left speechless when the
angels of the ninth day burst out of everyones chest."

¶ THE BUTTERFLY
EXPLOSION

Catch the electric picnic of vermilion snow
and celestial blue.

Look. See.

Tiny rainbows somersault from their diving-
board leaves all by themselves now, while
the cobalt wands of the wizard trees spark in
magenta and burnt marmalade.

Pink orchid clouds flutter by and smile, the
deepest gaze of stone and violet eyes stare from
the shooting stars as they elegantly tunnel their
meandering way through air avenues of light.

Just don't close your eyes or you will miss their
moonstone wings dripping in strawberry and
lilac spice.

See, it's happening all over again, the siren
waterfall of jade magnificence is showering her
glacial blue song, a solar hymn humming in
this forest explosion of night-sleepers.

Look. See.

Their little wings lead to everywhere that is
still.

¶ EVERYTHING IS STILL

Petals thunder as they
hit the forest floor.

A twig snaps underfoot
and the earth quakes.

A soft wind fondles the leaves
as a shy lightning unzips the sky.

A nightingale drinks from a gurgling stream
and a glacier breaks into her ancient song.

A moonbeam wakes a smooth pebble
and a storm of mountains rise to kiss the sky.

A drop of rain runs down my cheek
and I drown in a thousand oceans of glory.

¶ A LITTLE TRUTH

Truth is against the world,
but people could use a little shaking up
from time to time.

What's wrong with a little truth?

Maybe not too much to start with,
just a thimble-full to embellish our
momentous perceptions—like micro poetry
or flash fiction, nothing too deep or profound.

We don't want our flawless world to come
crashing down like a house of cards.
A little is a good start to
spyglass our lurking beauty.

After all, we are clearly doomed with our
daily koans running wild across
our steel cities of wish and whim.
A little truth, inflamed and urgent,
flurried and strange, may be just what
we need.

Our tiny kindergarten kingdoms

seem so sudden,

as if they were all just there.

Unforeseen,

swift, and

terribly nervous.

Don't you think?

We maybe a little

pretentious,

distracted, and

alarmed,

forever trying to stop time and

all those busy preparations for death.

Then along comes truth and she blows

into our lungs of stone and we stare

back at her, grey-faced, with our

boney shoulders and thin lips.

We thought her strange and grotesque,

yet it was wonderful how she

blew out all the monstrous things

that lean out of us from the shadows.

¶ THE SEA IS BEAUTIFULLY
STILL

I am flawed and perfect.

I know descent and ascent.

I am an ancient debut

desperately trying to hold myself together

for a few moments more.

I am complex. I grieve. I recover. I smile again.

I am a shifting wave, yet deeper the sea is still.

I am mortal, yet I burn like the stars.

I am more human than I think,

sculptured from an ancient earth magic.

I am more divine than I know,

see, my breath dances in the rare moonlight

unashamed and free.

¶ THE GEOGRAPHY OF THE
UNFAMILIAR

I asked for wonder, and an ocean roared
within my soul.

I asked to comprehend my soul, and I was
immediately filled with wonder.

I asked for speech to explain, and a poet's tear
formed inside my eye.

I asked for sight and I was made blind so I
could finally see.

I asked for answers and a vast forest of
questions rose high into the night sky.

I asked for light, and a thousand suns exploded
inside my chest.

I asked for reverence, and moonlight drowned
my pale cheeks.

I asked for love, and caught a sudden glimpse
of the abyss of God.

When I was in doubt I asked a hundred
questions; now I am in wonder I do not even
know how to ask the right question.

When I knew all things, I was certain and sure;
now I know nothing, I am simply aware and
amazed.

When I tried to write my destiny, I met
only despair; when I gave up the search, I
encountered the mystery as never before.

When I had creed and philosophy, I could
write a thousand books; now I am illiterate and
unwise, I can only write poetry about how the
moon-kissed ocean always carries me away.

Angry is just sad's bodyguard.

- Liza Palmer

Why yes, I am a poet and language is my weapon.

I sometimes duct tape shining sabers to my little wooden pencils as I write.

Other times the little wooden pencils are quite content to be wearing a white feather and garland of lavender.

I unfold a few lines, rehearse it to my often astonished face, and hope the big heart that I know you have, can read in-between all the erratic squiggles desperately wanting to be heard.

| *On My Poetry*

Opening up the mystic wonder of grace and love will make you think in mile-long poetry. At times it may seem just like a clutter of love and other wonderful feelings, other times it will be a thick and silent fog, but it is always a grand and wonder-filled tangle that is weaving light and beauty together on all the future pages of your life.

| *Mile-Long Poetry*

❡ SURREAL BREAKFAST
DECONSTRUCTED

No one noticed at first, but with a groan like a cello the weather changed direction just after three o'clock in the morning. The clouds took a monastic vow of artistic transformation that was about to rupture reality across the entire planet.

It came as no surprise that soon after I had risen, having caught the moon's final smiles waning in soft sunflower yellow, that something was not quite right. Something had changed, and to add to the gathering feelings of unease, I was hearing several small fluttering sounds, coming from where I did not exactly know.

Breakfast deconstruction begun early that morning.

The wind was not immune, it gave up its usual high moral ground of patrolling the earth and clanging the bells of monasteries hidden high up in the Himalayas. This morning it chose to incarnate itself in the small glass of fresh milk before me. The face of the wind carried a complexion of whites and browns with a smooth smile and a velvety cheek that could be seen when I held the glass up to the light.

The wind, now milk, was staring right back at me, and with a smirk once more.

"Expect a storm soon, kites will fly higher than ever before," it said with a rather nonchalant grin. It went back to swirling around in my glass, and with each revolution it winked a smile at me saying, "Expect a storm."

What was once known only hours before as 'air' or 'wind' seemed to be taking great delight in shattering all known laws of physics and my grip on sanity. It continued to wash the little white-water-sea up against the great transparent glass cliffs. The funny thing was, that with each wash of milk over the side of my glass, the splash never made it to the tabletop, instead, each droplet sprouted a pair of translucent wings and became like a small white butterfly that immediately headed towards my half open kitchen window never to be seen again.

I stood there, at a complete lost for words, when the toaster went 'pop'.

I glanced over, but no toaster could be seen on my bench; instead, a rather plump and fluffy white owl was pacing quickly back and forth. He kept shrugging his dumple-white shoulders, ruffled his thick neck, and stretched one foot, and then the other. Waddling along my kitchen bench he was chattering about a myriad of things that were, according to him, 'running amok' on the planet.

"This world is movin' much faster now, yes, yes, yes, much faster now—and the seagulls, oh yes, yes, yes, they are going to be twice their size and probably just as frustrated at their lack of food."

Having already deep misgiving as to what was happening in my kitchen this morning, things grew even more bizarre. My bowl of porridge quickly gathered itself into a rather odd arrangement of soggy clumps. A surface skin began congealing from the milky mix, terraforming what could only be described as tiny islands, complete with forests and rivers and mountains. Forming before my eyes was an entire ecosystem in my normally plain cereal bowl. The owl said it was experiencing some sort of 'realignment and rebirth'. Adding to the confusion, the sugar I had sprinkled only moments before began to rise up out of the bowl creating a miniature bluster of nimbostratus cloud formations. Several seconds later these clouds began to drizzle an orange rain just near the center of the newly formed land mass.

My slices of peeled apple, once sitting so peacefully on my plate, had melted into a small lake of bright blue water that swirled around and around the saucer, as if caught in a little cosmic whirlpool. It was then that the white owl (yes, the one that was a toaster only moments before) began to address me in an unmistakable Irish accent.

"Top of the morn' to you. Now don't you go to gettin' all worried and the like—tis only that all things are startin' to return to their pure essence. Everythin' is shifting to an alternate reality—to more than life, aye. Everythin' is changin' now. Rearrangin'. Revolvin'. Everythin' that can be shaken is gonna be shaken, includin' you.

I almost sensed a slight patronage in his voice as his head tilted slowly to one side.

"And about time too," said the white owl, "everythin' is not as it seems—nor has it ever been as it seems." He paused briefly, looked at the white butterfly-like creatures heading to the window and then whispered, "Look, there is a multiverse of aboreal creatures about to make a sudden appeerence on your planet and I am sure every pine cone in your mind will fight against what you see."

"What on earth do you mean," I asked, mocking myself at even the thought of having responded to this odd and cocky creature.

"Well," he continued, ruffling his feathers, "things are beginning to lose their previous state: the wind, the porridge, even the moon and stars, they are all tired of being misunderstood, and all those little crystal cubes of sugar, they 'av always been anxious to reveal some deeper cosmic meaning to life. But other than that everythin' is just fine… though you do look more than a little perplexed if I can say so."

"Perplexed? More like terrified, what on earth is happening—and what have you done to my toaster?"

The white owl stopped, tilted its feathery head to the other side, and looked directly at me as it tapped one of its little claws on the marble bench top.

"Well isn't it obvious?" He pronounced those words with a slow relish.

"All of life is interdependent and you have all been livin' as if you were the only ones in existence. So this mornin' just after three o'clock the wind, the moon, and all manner of created things took a vow and decided to surprise every soul who wakes up early and heads for breakfast this fine morn'. Aye, yes, clouds, water, wind, minerals, metals, moonlight, porridge, toasters, and even us owls—we all conspired to shake the existing quantum paradigms in a one grand display of utter non-scientific oddity and befuddlement."

"But I still don't understand," I asked, feeling like a complete imbecile making such a fuss over talking owls, flying milk, and sugar clouds raining orange juice.

The white owl flew over to the table and perched on the chair opposite me as several more milky white flying things found their winged freedom towards the approaching dawn.

"Somethin' had to break all the allergies you humans have—you're all got addictions to certain beliefs, you all 'av a thirst for violence and meanness; all your superstitions, your collective hallucinations, and especially all those trite clichés of neurotic individualism—aye, ya peoples minds are a bit daft, filled with everythin' but the truth."

"Truth!" I laughed, trying to ignore the chaffing nature of those last remarks. "But I am talking to an owl with an Irish lilt whilst a new planet is forming in my porridge bowl. How can you talk to me about truth?"

But the owl did talk—on and on he went for almost another twenty minutes. He spoke of tribalism, of fanaticism, of nationalism, of racism, and even religious fundamentalism and how the human mind is obsessed with a vast array of manufactured desires that keep causing untold havoc the world over. He kept on using phrases I never thought existed in such simple creatures, words such as 'mass-drift psychosis', 'reality distortion', 'unholy alienation', and 'chaos shadows'. Finally, he ended his philosophical discourse muttering about how he had nowhere to build a decent nest in the midst of all this great confusion.

Then, as if the creature had a thousand ideas all at once, the owl flew to my nearby bookshelf, took my old copy of Mary Shelley's *Frankenstein* in its tight claw and dropped it in front of me. He flicked it open with his beak and his right claw tapped the first page.

"Look 'ere—this is what is about to happen to your kind all over…"

He started to read swaying back and forth in a slow dancing rhythm.

I listened to his words, whilst every part of my face wondered aloud at the fact that owls could read publically in the first place.

"I shall satiate my ardent curiosity with the sight of a part of the world never before visited, and may tread a land never before imprinted by the foot of man. These are my enticements, and they are sufficient to conquer all fear of danger or death and to induce me to commence this laborious voyage with the joy a child feels when he embarks in a little boat..."

"Are you ready?"

"Ready for what," I cried.

"Ready to gain a sight of a world you've never visited before."

The white owl paused momentarily as its dark, wide-moon eyes blinked at me.

"You're goin' upriver in that little boat laddy, yes, yes—way, way upriver, further than you have ever gone before. In your current state of amazement you suppose that all I have spoken to be nothing but conjecture and false tidings. You think I am an embellishment of some approaching insanity, a spark of dreamy madness, a figment of your bewildered imagination. Ah, but just you wait, your soul will scarce believe the wonders that are comin'. If I revealed any more at this stage you would not be able to comprehend even the smallest of phrases. You've all been used to puddles your whole life long, but somethin', and may I add that it could be very soon, is going to plunge you to a depth of existence far greater than ever before. You have merely experienced a thimble-sea you call the Pacific, wait till that is held in the palm of your hand."

꒰ WHEN WILL I LET GO OF
MY EYES

All beings are incredibly beautiful.

All souls are infinitely precious.

It is a terrifying fire millions cannot see.

Could I hold you and shake you

into this flame of sight?

Maybe it will show you something

wonderful about the darkness.

And if I fail, then slowly, in time,

something helpless within you

will hunger for this great sight.

Till then, warm your naked

and cold bones before the

glowing embers of the

soul of the universe.

ꟼ A SMALL ANTHOLOGY OF
DELIGHTFUL SORROW

I have a mouthful of panic, frantic lists, and questions.

I am a deer trapped in the headlight rush of oncoming reality.

Tranquil oblivion is not an option, nor can despair be quietly muffled by a few extra pillows, so I will stand still, alone in the bright light, paralyzed as all the flowers shout my apocalyptic name from the roadside next to me.

The ineffable moon has a long and patient smile, it enters the soul like a slow bullet.

A shock to delicate tissue everywhere, harrowing the reason, enflaming the dark— soulshock is deadly real.

The night sky goes on for miles and miles, and I wonder where I misplaced the thin cellophane.

I might need it to fix the gash in my soul, the wind is rushing in and the light is pouring out.

I am helpless, knowing that my body is not my own, nor my soul.

Self is jealous. I was happily infatuated with me the way I was; but now I break, I am pounded with something reckless and free.

Chaos Spirit. Your brooding has an intricate order, it is the eighth chakra disguised as wind, with eyes of fire and words as rain.

You live among the whirlwinds and rest in rib-caves everywhere.

Your wind whistles among the needles of the tall pines. Souls, like leaves, shimmer at the forest so full of life.

The milk-blue sky ripples in all directions as it collides with God within—is it any wonder I cannot stand?

There are words in life so powerful that entire worlds are formed in their speaking. They have a wild face, full of unraveling sonnets, closet wonders where lily and lotus bloom.

Haven't you yet heard, deconstruction lasts longer than a single day. One cannot expect to find a valley full of rainbows in a single step—or can you?

¶ HOW TO BE A HAPPY POET

On a windy day stay balanced on the fragile
tightrope and don't overuse verbs that demand
their own way with you.

Don't assassinate other poets while they are in
dialogue with the ocean.

Wear comfortable clothes, especially if lost in a
library.

Don't have an anxiety attack over English
grammar and broken wooden pencils.

Remember, muse is microscopic. It begins
its nanite swarm when ideas collide in the
cloudscapes of your soul.

Moonstones are magic, so are blades of grass,
forest dew, and still lakes with white swans, but
don't expect them all to talk at once.

If you are stuck in northern Europe in the
nineteenth century, try and find a little
wooden elf with a red quill, he will know what
to do.

When you sit down to write, expect the
unexpected, every single time—and above all
things: keep listening for trapped voices.

Beginnings tend to break up into small
fragments that float through the air and land
in the tin cup sitting on your desk—rattle it if
you are in doubt, something healing may just
tumble out.

Read other peoples words that are very unlike yours. Read other peoples words that are very much like yours.

Enjoy a literary hug when it comes, the difference in emotional temperature is due to the fact that our planet is sometimes tilted on its axis towards the moon. Some poets see it, some don't.

When the world goes to war, write a poem. When the world comes to its senses, write two more.

Trees are still incredibly popular with angels, go and sit under one and thank the forest for all the green word paint right at your finger-tips. Remember, the fluttering of wings may not always be birds.

If you ever manage to walk on the sun, collect a pocket full of sparks. When you return to earth begin to write words that start fires.

Writing poetry is like a polite Japanese girl in her early twenties, sometimes she blushes in her silk kimono and bows her head among the cherry blossoms.

When waiting for a poem; breathe, wait, and wait a little longer. If it's cold outside, wait for the sky—the soft white, the splash of clouds, the long gaze of winter, even the littlest droplet of rain. These can all bring a cool cargo from the heavens and drip it inside your window-staring soul.

The slowest creature on earth is the three-toed sloth—sometimes your inspiration is as faithfully unenergetic as its top speed, depressing isn't it.

Static words hackle you from the corner of your barren page, but often you will see a bright blue spark in their eyes. Resist the urge to punch them in the face, be gentle.

You are amphibious: you can go beyond the shore, beyond the land—you can climb into outer space and drink herbal tea with the stars.

ꝰ TREE POETRY

The small silk leaves wear little gowns of
starlight ready to drink the night.

The high dark twigs breathe out a special kind
of magic, a cloud-finger cosmology prying
meaning from the air.

A grain of sand awaits the voice of a
moonbeam to start singing her liquid hymn of
immersion.

A fallen leaf gathers what's left of her rain-
heart and insists she sleeps quietly in the shade
of her former palace walls.

A dandelion seed wraps himself in a tiny lace
parachute before he leaps into the next rush of
wind.

A long haired vine hugs her tree trunk tightly,
her heavy veined green fingers twitching in the
sea-breeze.

The green lips of the forest whisper stories
of pregnant wonders and sway gently until
evening.

The young roots stretch and yawn and settle
down for the next decade, the brown earth
rumbles a harmless smile.

And not too far away, the blue lipstick of the
ocean washes off when she kisses the white
cheeks of the shore.

Please, don't disturb the trees by the ocean,
they are writing poems that no one will ever
read.

¶ OPINION EX CATHEDRA

A poem on how we often gravitate to spiritual or intellectual arrogance, and when, as Maria Popova (Brainpickings) says, *"It's enormously disorienting to simply say, 'I don't know.' But it's infinitely more rewarding to understand than to be right—even if that means changing your mind about a topic, an ideology, or, above all, yourself."* We often form our opinions based on superficial impressions or the borrowed ideas of others, and then, with all the force of a small hurricane, blow their wild winds thinking they are *Ex Cathedra* to every soul on earth:

    I am a fluorescent social disgrace

    flashing my superficial light formed

    in the everlasting flicker of a neon time-god.

    I have stuffed my cavernous mind with

    the thud of years and borrowed ideas.

    I am crowned with a rusty iron halo,

    wreathed in a shroud of colossal intellect—

    the artistic anchors of my own reality form

    a globe-wrapping litany of blur and bluster.

    The grey ravens have landed,

    they have pecked away at my soul and

    left me to plod towards ideological captivity,

    a frozen rainbow lies shattered on

    the marble steps of my polemicist flare.

    I am stuck in a colorless land of

    twig and bramble.

    My avant-garde art of the shallow and

uninformed betrays a comprehensive bliss at

the margin of consciousness.

Endemic is my anecdotal legacy,

a cagey genius set free to stalk the

virginity of your gentle mind.

I am the center, the absolute,

and the only intensity.

I am the fingerprint of God

upon your soul—a burning bush

in your intellectual desert;

come, see how I burn and

apprehend the divine—

stain your fingers with my fire

and your black-tar eyes will

shine with psychic gold.

The love in you will observe and be moved
with compassion; it is all those preconditioned
thoughts, still not tamed by the wildfire of
divine love, which prefer to judge another soul
as unworthy. Love always kneels in the dust,
if need be, and says, "Neither do I condemn
you."

| *Unconditional*

I once read that, "I am a raging ocean trapped inside a raindrop." And I thought to myself; what a powerful metaphor of the glorious and wild beauty contained within the human soul. So much potential, freedom, life, and abundance—all waiting to break forth, but trapped, horridly trapped in our unbeliefs, doubts, and fears. If truth does set people free, then what is it that shall pierce that thin raindrop's translucent membrane? Long has the human soul suffered under gross materialism, ignorance, warfare, stupidity, arrogance, and everything else contrary to love. What is it that shall cause even a small trickle to flow into this eternal quality of life we are promised? Surely there must be some bridge from this inner world to the outer, and if there is, I want to discover it and drown in its torrential flow.

| *FLOW*

I have come into this world to see this: the
sword drop from men's hands even at the
height of their arc of anger because we have
finally realized there is just one flesh to wound.

| *HAFIZ*

Oceans roar, mountains rumble, the great
forests of earth sway in storms that shake their
every limb. The rains fall, the winds blow,
and a gentle dew trickles down some blade
of grass no living soul will ever see. Planets
dance their kaleidoscopic waltz, moons spin
and disappear around their dance-floor orbits.
And somewhere out in silence a star explodes
in the vastness of space, shaking millions of
miles of nothing, and here—here on this tiny
planet someone called Earth I am worried
about finding a parking space. When will I be
anchored in what really matters? When shall
awe imprison me? When will love consume
me? I believe *love* is still the greatest force in
the entire universe. And I don't think someone
was just waxing all poetic when they once said,
"God *is* love." And whatever God is (and we
have been given plenty of clues), God is always
and irrevocably, *love*.

| *THE ORBIT OF LOVE*

¶ INCISION

Why does a sword beam of
sharp marble moonlight
conceal her gentle incision
upon the silver surface
of my soul?

Why do the creeping
margins of a grey
and leafless world seem
a little less helpless now?

Why does the white blade sink deep,
past soil skin and bone trees,
finally coming to rest upon a glowing sun
beating in a fiery meadow at
the center of everything?

Darkness cannot endure the night,
and a curfewed black sky
will always bow silently
before the cloudless inner storm
of the sun.

Who can ever survive the
drenched white brilliance of
a moon-lance upon the
bare earth of the soul.

¶ PROBABLY A POET

I am a hermit in a forest of moon-kissed paper
leaves.

I am myth, fable, and imagination prowling
the dead regions of unknown soulscapes.

I am exotic, extinct, caught between the living
and the dead, and I always want to talk about
the whispering trees.

I am silverware polished until they gleam in
the dark all by themselves.

I am a natural bayonet, velvet chromed,
capturing air dreams from the corner of my
eye.

I breach the protocols of vocabulary and crack
the Plexiglass barrier with comets forged from
forgotten ink.

I loop across the world with filial reverence
and awful piety; an interwoven rainbow as
lavish as the sun.

I own a magic shop with a maze of stairs
winding to wonder.

I am a tummy bulge on the virgin belly of the
universe.

I am a brave and wise companion that will fill
your gaze with tears and light.

I am probably a poet.

ꝑ WILDFLOWER SOUL AND THE SCALPEL

I saw an angel sifting through the trash
looking for a bottle of sacramental vision.

I thought I would be a gentle god and offer
him new wings made of leaves and water.

He looked at me, smiled, and shot skyward,
like reverse lightning, a thread of silver light to
a passing cloud.

It seems the cold night holds light in an
imprisoned state—unshaven angels can fall
and rise with the best of us.

I have so many questions about paradise.

I don't want a splash of golden lipstick
dripping from the honey lips of the latest
televangelist—I don't need any more ice picks
to my soul, where the mountain tops billow
and howl.

In this exhilarating universe, reverse angels fly
between oblivion and meaning. I wonder if I
will ever find my way back home or will the
moon collapse in front of my astonished eyes
and sing her final earth eulogy without a drop
of light?

Sister moon, fill me with a liquid incision—
drown me, bloom in me, raise me to your
white light mouth and be a river of fire in me.

Carve me a lute from a willow tree, lay my
sylvan soul in a glade of flowers and hold my
trembling hand—help me locate silence and I
shall sing poetry carved from silk.

¶ THE MYSTIC

And the mystic played long into the night on his wooden flute, allowing his imagination to become both fire and light that danced about his soul:

> The volcanic forge of love. Soul fury. A secret place of beauty. A deep invitation, stillness.
>
> Silence unveils a deep shroud. The mystic is undone, caught seeing in the blindness of great-sight.
>
> Thunderstorm mountains gather inside the heart to breath a glory out of repeated chaos.
>
> A web of light tightens. Blood is fire, breath is ocean, mind is moonlight. Unknowing is a thorn upon the soul.
>
> The chest burns lung-fulls of awe, glowing embers glimmer like starving paupers before a thousand suns.
>
> Some words are too huge to allow anything else to breath besides them. A window opens and is enfolded by poetry.
>
> There is so much beauty…in the world— an entire life lies behind things, a deeper conversation speaking a benediction beyond all endings.
>
> Wreathed in blue where there is no plateau, the ascending fire of primeval ground washes with rain and wind, cradling a voyage into the vast unknown.
>
> Sacred emptiness fills with divine fullness. The embrace begins, sheltered in an ultimate infusion of grace.

A conspiracy of the trees, a deception of the oceans—dark valleys, towering peaks, grief and bliss, and beyond all that: abiding stillness.

Unforeseen things emerge as a brush touches a white canvas, its strokes are fiercely free in the grip of some new wine symmetry. The art of the symbiotic circle of undreaming.

At the edge of night pound waves of darkness. At the edge of light wash waves of brightness. The rush of so many mysteries.

Belonging to the soul of the earth, remembering the name of the sky, at rest in the womb of the world.

An invisible geography, disturbing everything, the paradox of a hundred sorrows emerging towards transformation of being.

Thought gives birth to new colors on the shore of dawn. On the wings of mystery is both outer immensity and inner infinity.

Unmoored and lost in the deep abyss of God. The fall into love, each soul a different shape sheltered in a secret universe of drowning.

The absolute stillness of a divine hurricane. A beautiful violence, a sacred peace, a requiem twilight, a sensuous sight.

The soul crisis of a heart haunted with a mind madness. The ache and longing for an eternal rest that is stilled only with a *oneing*.

Immortal belonging begets an intimacy with all beings. The urgency of compassion begins its slow burn.

Unbearable is this land of dead poetry that
can find no words of resurrection. Homeless
and demented in the temple of abandoned
self-expression. There is no peace for the over-
saturated mind, the breathless voice, and the
empty tongue.

The winds of destiny no longer blow. How can
they in the place where I am everywhere and
nowhere all at once.

Rooted forever in the forest of the universe.
Lonesome veins can cease their striving, the
sap of divine nectar streams within their
branches.

Air, the breath of God. Water, the tears of
earth. Fire, the essence of soul. Stone, the
temple of memory. The mystic horizon gathers
her skirt and runs to greet me.

Gentle slope of unfolding flowers, why are you
all ablaze in the breeze of burning rain? The
elements are become one.

Bodhisattvas and Messiahs adorned in purple-
spiced robes; the night decays, the morning
comes. The blackness of the sun has seen a
great light.

The sun behind the sun, the moon behind the
moon, the cloudless night—Oh soul, look up
into heaven and laugh...laugh at the bright air,
the fertile earth, the summit of eyes beholding
a door not of this world.

And the mystic played long into the night on his wooden flute, allowing
his exhausted memories to dance on and on till he was seen no more.

¶ POETIC DISSONANCE

"Where does creativity come from?"

"Creativity comes from the *Forge of Everywhere*, the breath of music and art and poetry is wrapped in the Universe itself."

"But I feel all my words never seem to land on their own two feet. They leap naked on their postmodern languagescape, often burrowing in shame beneath spiritual voice-prints that wanted way too much — I feel they remain numb, aloof, shivering from standing out in the cold rain for too long."

"You know you have permission."

"Permission for what?"

"Permission to spark and flare. Create whatever you want. Creativity flows through us all, urging us to move beyond the perceived edge of what we think will pop and fizz in the great conscious muddle of the masses. Whether your words are formed down in the moon grotto or up in the sun clouds, give them the magic of flight."

"But how can I kindle this incantatory flame? Surely there is a place where all those sought after sonic glyphs fall into new narrative spaces. I want them to be at once both urgent and magnificent, erudite and complex, yet simple and free."

"From the way you are speaking I do not see what your problem is, but remember society is so fragmented and eclectic — someone,

somewhere will absolutely love your work.
Language is golden in color, delicious in taste,
an organism alive with an ascending flame,
like a mythical firebird returning to the sun.
Allow your soul to enlarge and escape."

"And how do I do that?"

"Do what?"

"Allow my soul to enlarge and escape."

"I have absolutely no idea."

❡ THE DAY GOD DIED

God is surrounded by ten-thousand stern faced angels. They do not know how to smile—abandoning their harps and flutes long, long ago. They grip their iron-grey wings with clenched fists as their once golden-hair crumbles to the stone floor like soot.

Vast stained glassed windows tower overhead. The great celestial throne room lay still, like a blister. The air rippled as frost flashed down every corridor—a chilling gush of wind moaned its long hymn over the hard marble floors. An angel stared at me and shadowed a cruel smile.

Then God died.

Ten-thousand angels also.

The universe mourned.

Churches closed, mosques were abandoned, synagogue candles gave no more light or flame. Monasteries fell silent, not even a temple bell could be heard chiming at the soft-fingered caress of the wind. All sentient life wrung their hands and threw dust high into the trembling face of the Milky Way.

All except one small yellow flower—she beamed for joy that morning, for she breathed in the very breath of God and wept in colors never seen before.

'mysterium tremendum et fascinans'

There is a transcendent Mystery before me which draws me, fills me, causes me to tremble and fascinates me no end. The way is narrow. My soul seems so thin. A mere membrane of light. But still too thick and wall-like to enter this region the Beautiful Enigma. All my necessary humility lies begging at the gate of a Sight Most Wonderful. I am starving, but full; poor, but rich beyond measure; empty, but overflowing; blind, but seeing; deaf, but hearing; held captive, but as free as the light from a thousand dancing stars. So why do I dread? Why do I fear? Why am I so in love? Why this double form of the sacred? Why the light and dark? Why this overpowering? Why this awe? Why this deadness within and without? Ah, beautiful nothingness I am, yet so full of everything. I no longer live, but somehow I do. I am in the guest-room of a paradox longing for a gentler heart. Is this a potent charm from an angel's wand? What wine is this that ripples ceaselessly in my inner sea? In the dead of night something crept in, lantern and dagger in hand, and cut open my soul and poured in a liquid light that made me catch afire. I am ruined, so wonderfully ruined, and none can help my hopeless burning now.

| Mysterium Tremendum

§ BUTTERFLY STORM

Like reckless little flames glinting wide smiles,
an orange rupture filled her evening sight
surrounding her forest hollow from
which she would simply sit and
look out through her thirsty eyes,
musing a kinder world.

This living, moving, burning cloud,
woven against air and earth,
with the smell of leaves and flowers
swirling and falling, each in a dance of
magnificent solitude—tiny capsules of
safety, light, and color became
open doorways to
a quieter radiance.

This palace of leaves and wind
built by a butterfly storm reminded her,
like a fragment from some forgotten conversation,
that she herself was being perceived by
the flames of green and gold and greatness.
It was a tranquillity that terrified her,
yet she felt inexplicably loved
and in love
with this nameless summer's eve
that poured continuously before her
like a burning waterfall.

¶ SWIMMING WITH ANGELS

It is time to burn down
the old dream world,
this cacophony of soul
forever roaring out its
desperate harvest.

My delight of technique.
The sandcastles of method.
The tug and shove of
darker desires growling out
their engine of rusty mists.

I am swimming with angels
and I am unaware, drowning in the
wash of their majestic wings?

Yet I am still tangled in a
fantastic harbor, leaden
in a sky of soaring ocean birds.

Despite all your topsy-turvy thoughts and jumbled spirituality you can still experience deep joy in the midst of a sea of vast contradictions. This is the embrace of the mystical, the paradox of the unexplained, and the golden glove of silent unanswered questions. You're desperate to 'go and figure it all out', but the more you do, the more muddled you become, until you finally realize the deep things of your soul need only to find the still waters of an eternal rest.

In ideologies there is no tenderness, no love, no meekness. And ideologies are rigid, always set in solid concrete and oxygen starved. When a soul becomes a disciple of an ideology, he has lost the faith: he is no longer a disciple of the fire of love—he has become a disciple of a mere attitude or thought. Ideology may purport to know a great many things, but it actually has very few things worth knowing. The knowledge of wisdom is seduced into an ideological and moralistic pseudo-knowledge that closes the door with its many conditions. When faith, hope and love become an ideology it breeds fear. Ideology frightens, ideology chases away people, it distances, separates, and alienates. Ideology hates questions and areas of doubt, it delights to enforce, despises gentleness and kindness, and will ultimately kill for God, country, or self, if need be.

| *Oxygen Starved*

¶ HONESTY WITHOUT
LEAKAGE

"I don't live like a poet," I once said, "nor do I look like one, but I know the words of trembling prophets are still written on subway walls and rarely in the stadium halls, cheering fans swooning, smoke and noise booming, and that forever arduous and necessary soul-smirk of ego."

"I don't think like a poet," I once said, "nor do I write like one, but I trust my words are direct, open, simple, strangely hospitable, sensuous, and earthy—that among their hallowed breathings, even their anger and lament, a ladder to the savage pull of moonlight still beckons."

"I don't hope like a poet," I once said, "nor do I dream like one, but as the next ferocious shipment of history arrives in its tattered and bruised boxes will it be full of good intent? Of hope or fear? Will I finally get to cross the deep ravine of tears that keep rushing between the broken sobs of what I thnk already is."

"I don't bleed as a poet," I once said, "nor do I cry a poet's tears, but the severity of an unearthly compassion stands as an allusive fire before me—naked, yet crystalline, culturally dangerous with its reverent knife edge refusing to dance in the muscular neon light of conquering trendy religion."

"I don't speak like a poet," I once said, "nor do I feel like one, but my strange analogies quarrel and twist away at my soul with its rusty halo and simple childhood ways. The old prophets? They lie on their side in a fetal position, curled and burning, their bellies aflame with something from the root of all trees, something primal, something undivided and yearning to be free."

"I don't breathe like a poet," I once said, "nor will I die like one, but the desert sky is partially clear tonight as it passes overhead, squeezing out its unlikely droplets of awe kissed by wonder. These thawing stars are hyphens, small lifelines holding out an angel's voice, a crease in a cosmos unfinished, buried deep in the mercy of meaning—and I alone stumble forward, still not listening to the irony of an unfolding that no one ever dares pay any attention to."

¶ THE SLOW-BREATHING CIRCUS

I wish to give wings my soul.

To attend a victory far from the world maze moaning out desperate hymns in the oblivion rush of long night.

I am sure some gods disappear and become uninvented, united in a worshipless non-existence, orphan deities starved in the holocaust of time and the aftershocks of a Paradise lost.

And the atheist sits and invokes the gods he never believes in. "We must purge them from our grammar," he says.

And the priest sits and does the same with a liturgy of spiritual clichés set to beautiful song.

Oh stoic soul, probing, spiritually ambidextrous, wondering why pain lurks in the lines of poetry no one will ever read.

This is a slow breathing circus, surrounded by a fateful language hiding in smog, a desperate pun seeking out meaning.

The comical and the tragic seem to attend all the forbidden feasts set in honor of dead gods sitting in the dark corners of the room.

I rebel, only a little, playfully at first, for the horror of a soul vacuum brings no equilibrium. I wait for love to gently pry open my withering head.

Reverence still rubs away at my edges, an elegy of defiance refusing to depart.

I want to do something I don't know how to do—I want to hog all the love in the universe for myself. Is it no surprise then that my narcissistic soul lights up like a switchboard full of blasphemous electricity?

I say a prayer. Choric fatalism? Reflexive doubt? I create my personal religious zone. I pray for the dead—laying sepulcher brick upon brick, first for myself and then the ghost of a God creeping in the shadows of my soul.

Anguish provokes me as a sweet world is soaked in wine. Why do complications always embrace a strange and wild freedom? I am a soldier-poet and my words are full of religious strife seeking an everywhere peace all-at-once.

I scream inside and whisper quietly that everything is okay.

I read the modern prophets: a mix of sorrow and sorrow with a cheeky grin, happiness dressed in perfumed rags, little girls holding wilting flowers, little boys stepping on broken glass. Don't they notice their feet are bleeding?

I am in motion. A form of spiritual tropism, white-light dependent, tumbling downside-up, perhaps for the very first time. I'm germinating an embryo in my male womb. I feel the kick inside, and living waters ripple across my belly.

Even the wind and the sparrows know that nothing is hopeless. Fading eyesight doesn't mean you stop seeing. I am learning to resee from my lockjaw life. I am learning to slow breathe in the midst of a temple dedicated to the wonder of everything.

⸮ THE DEATH OF A
BUTTERFLY

Quiet light-wings in a final fold,

her little silken head gently bows.

All her primordial defenses are down.

The rush of a thousand burning arrows

dance in the violet twilight.

A veiling now unveiling.

Exhausted she rests atop a

mountain of lavender and lilac.

Her tiny soul clogged by abundance.

Every particle of her breath-like world aflame.

The butterfly staggers at the silent

tidal wave of beauty now rushing towards her.

You may cry in your handkerchief,

sigh out a grieving bag of swords,

nod and close your teary eyes in

a sympathetic meditation,

but if you remain very still you

will see a small halo dissolving

into a meadow of blooming flowers

all swaying in their green and gold silk dresses.

"Why of all days must I be here?"

And she will sing to you from her

final breath of gold and white:

"Today I am become a bouquet of
velvet thunderbolts—an intense
light gathering around your aching
soul, an awakening jolt from one
you considered very weakness itself.
Though you are darkened with fear
in the garden of beasts, you will find
that even the blackest of souls
can feast on light and
become radiant."

ꝯ A WALK THROUGH A
GRAVEYARD

The stone angels are barking like
dogs in the white tulip grove,
their voices trampling the sorrow flowers
and their fading lilac scent—they
don't really care
about inner care
after all.
And I think to myself:
How does one go about dying?
I am especially curious if anyone
has ever walked this way before
and figured out a way to avoid this
final tumble into unspoiled oblivion?

Before I gift my soul to the sky,
before I stir the leaves and wild flowers with
my breathless-flesh form, I wonder if the tall oaks
will tell me their old mysteries—of the silent earth,
of the ash-grey realm, of the white noose of stillness,
and of what really lies under that great knot of damp soil?
'You trees have drunk the nectar of mystery for centuries,
surely there is bread and wine for the likes of me.'
Restlessly turning in my long shadow bed, my
Eucharist body lies broken on the cracked steps of time,

I will dip my brittle quill into the brown earth and write a
final poem to guide you through the asphyxiating
fog of a new world gathering.

The stone angels are howling now, like moon dogs,
snapping a cruel grin with each sweep of
their monstrous granite wings. They clamor across
the manicured lawns, kicking up dust in the shadows,
grey-bone prophets sporting a sandstone stare,
cacophonous words slapping about my ears.

I want to know if this purple bruise of a soul
will ascend like burning sage or a lavender liturgy?
Will I roam in the fresh fields of a virgin universe,
star bright, with real meaning dilating my wide ocean eyes,
a splash of myth and magic, magnificence and more?

But the blessed burning neon lights
unravel their methamphetamine glow,
they are sure to drip like warm molasses
all over my little paper-paradise mind, the
flashbulb chantings of society never tire,
nor restrain in
honoring the fleeting,
burning incense to the eternally mundane.
Give us this day our daily breath
for tomorrow is the madness,

the cold gust, and the dread.

How soon I forget the sheer velocity of life,

romanced with the flirting sensations

that I am somehow, bravely immortal.

I wonder if my soul will be a cesarean delivery

into the fields and woods of the world to come?

I don't want to deliver myself, struggle and gasp,

with a giant push through the tight fjords of eternity,

their high stone walls with staring angels in

celestial array—no, I want to be cut through,

pulled out by a gentle hand, guided by

a hymn of love purring softly in the distance.

Will I rise out of the ash?

Will I be wiser?

Will I be kinder when I awake?

Will my eyes be filled with ancient fire?

Or will I be gentle like a radiant moon

hovering over the mists of Venus?

I will have a long conversation on my first evening,

the leading edge of divine discovery cannot be a

hollow library full of wordless books and empty minds.

This is the anteroom of creation and shining souls,

surely we can talk mystery long into the night before the

burning glow of a tumbling nebula.

¶ STARLEAF

Falling star or falling leaf—both burn with a single magnificence, there is no difference to the seeing. The timid soul first discovers her name is of fire, then you hear her silent roar, her ocean of thunder, her intensity and joy, then a longing to dance alone with the trees.

So dance O wild-flower soul, dance with the moonlight burning her gentle breath across your wild hair. The forest itself will rise to meet you; even her breathings seem to know that your life and every life is part of this *one* great awakening cry.

The soul is unbreakable, but she can be broken.

The soul is untouchable, but she can be hurt and lost in the mire of life.

The soul is indestructible, but she is soon trampled upon like a delicate flower.

One thing I am aware of more than ever is that during the process of deconstruction and the reconstruction of new belief we become fragile. We can become bruised with all the books, all the learning, and all the unlearning. We enter a twilight realm of soul—an unsleeping. Not yet awake, but not now asleep. We know well the storms of questions rushing through us as we attempt to make sense of a whole range of issues. So tread carefully; be gentleness, be kindness, and be compassion—both with others and with yourown heart. For you are carrying within you a sacred spring, a watered womb, an aperture that you do not yet realize will flood your thirsty world with light. Cultivate the heart of your forest instead of trying to burn it down with all those hot and aggressive flashes that demand so much more than what you are prepared to give at the moment.

| UNBREAKABLE, BUT BROKEN

The earth tremors from her deep story. And what of this thing called consciousness? It is the fire inside the soul of the whole world— and within us. The mystics get it, everyone one else fights about it. We become alive with all our plunging and delving into this deep mystery.

Welcome then to the psychic rupture of your eternal boredom. You cannot fall out of the ever watchful eye of glowing moons and burning suns, you can only go deeper into their strange and magnificent light. Have no fear, they will continue to rip apart the thin stitches of your already frayed reality. The virgin maidens of wisdom and beauty wouldn't have it any other way, loving to see that tear in your eye that speaks of a deeper diamond peace, greater than all the moon-silver dew of a moon weeping for joy.

| *The Rupture*

Printed in Great Britain
by Amazon